ARCHANES

ISBN 960-213-234-5

Prof. J. A. SAKELLARAKIS Dr. E. SAPOUNA - SAKELLARAKI

ARCHANES

ARCHANES EXCAVATIONS
Prize of the Academy of Athens
1983

EKDOTIKE ATHENON S.A.
Athens 1991

Publishers: G.A. Christopoulos, J.C. Bastias

Managing Editor: Anna Mihopoulou
Translation: David Turner
Art Director: Tonia Kotsoni
Photography: Elias Eliades
Graphic Reconstructions: Stam. Vassiliou - E. Sakellaraki,
R. Oikonomakis (15), N.Giannadakis (119, 123, 125)
Phototypesetting: G. Athanasiou
Colour Separations: S. Papadopoulos - K. Alexandris LTD.

Printed by Ekdotike Hellados S.A.

CONTENTS

INTRODUCTION

ARCHANES AND CRETAN CIVILIZATION

In recent years, Archanes has come to rank amongst the foremost archaeological sites of Greece, traversing as it does all the stages of pre-historic Minoan civilization as well as those of historical times. The length of the site's inhabitation both as a settlement and as a venue for worship, not to mention its use as a burial centre, renders Archanes an integrated unity wherein all the forms and activities of one of Crete's most important communities – including both centre and hinterland – are represented over time.

The Neolithic Period (6000-2800 B.C.)

No phases older than the Neolithic period have been uncovered in Crete till now. From 6000 B.C., however, Neolithic civilization spread throughout the island. Initially, Neolithic settlements had the character of places of refuge in caves, which were also used as burial sites. Later, however, people settled in more permanent houses built of mud brick and stone. Weaving began to develop as did land cultivation accompanied by food gathering, while animal husbandry grew parallel to hunting. In the first phases of the Neolithic period, only Knossos is known to have been inhabited, but towards the end of the period the building of houses spreads throughout the island.

At Archanes, the first traces of human activity occur at the end of the Late Neolithic period and then through Sub-Neolithic times. A Neolithic axe was found at Vathypetro in the vicinity of the site; while closer by, at the Stravomyti cave, the first human dwellings have been uncovered and dated to this period. This data is clear proof that scattered communities existed at Archanes during the Late Neolithic and Sub-Neolithic periods but, on the other hand, cannot be taken to prove widespread settlement.

The Prepalatial Period (2800-2000 B.C.)

After 2800 B.C., bronze was imported into the Aegean, thus revolutionizing the till-then paltry technology of the Neolithic period. This change can also be observed in the Cyclades and mainland Greece and has been associated with the arrival of a new people or peoples. Crete now begins to establish contacts with Egypt, the East, and the Aegean islands; raw materials were imported in return for agricultural goods, and even works of fine craftsmanship.

Architecture during this period is characterized by sturdy buildings constructed with stones and mud bricks, while the common type of funerary structure can be found in the tholos tombs of Archanes and the Messara, the chamber tombs at Mochlos and the grave enclosures found at both Mochlos and Archanes. Meanwhile, caves and local shrines provided the venue for cult practices.

Traces of Early Minoan (henceforth EM) occupation were found in Archanes, at the Vorna site near the palace building, and so- called Vasiliki ceramic ware was found at the centre of the modern town (the Papadaki bakery site) as well as in Tour-koyeitonia underneath the later palace (Grivaki site). EM pottery has also been found in the eastern-most part of the town (Troullos). These four «islands» within the town delineate the area taken up by the EM settlement.

In the hinterland around Archanes, EM III pottery was found on the Vitsila site, while that at the Stravomyti cave is also considered as having been inhabited during this period, especially during EM II

1. The central part of the village of Archanes, framed by the wooden grape stacks, or krevatines.

CHRONOLOGICAL CHART
OF THE ANCIENT HISTORY OF CRETE

	Acc. to Evans	Acc. to Platon
5000 B.C.	NEOLITHIC ERA	NEOLITHIC ERA
2600 B.C.		
	EARLY MINOAN I EARLY MINOAN II EARLY MINOAN III MIDDLE MINOAN Ia	PRE-PALACE PERIOD
2000 B.C.		
	MIDDLE MINOAN Ib MIDDLE MINOAN IIa MIDDLE MINOAN IIb	OLD PALACE PERIOD
1700 B.C.		
	MIDDLE MINOAN IIIa, b LATE MINOAN Ia LATE MINOAN Ib LATE MINOAN II	NEW PALACE PERIOD
1400 B.C.		
	LATE MINOAN IIIa LATE MINOAN IIIb LATE MINOAN IIIc	POST-PALACE PERIOD
1100 B.C.		
	SUB-MINOAN – PROTO-GEOMETRIC PERIOD	
900 B.C.		
	GEOMETRIC PERIOD	
725 B.C.		
	ORIENTALIZING PERIOD	
650 B.C.		
	ARCHAIC PERIOD	
500 B.C.		
	CLASSICAL PERIOD	
330 B.C.		
	HELLENISTIC PERIOD	
67 B.C.		
	GRAECO-ROMAN PERIOD	
323 A.D.		

and III. Finally, Sir Arthur Evans collected EM pottery from the Karydaki site. Thus we know that the area was inhabited at a very early stage.

The cemetery at Phourni, however, provides us with a more complete picture of the organization of the settlement itself, whose architectural remains were lost under later buildings. Evidence for the wealth of the inhabitants is provided by the cemetery's carefully planned funerary buildings, particularly those from the EM II period, which in addition to giving up a host of pottery also provided many funerary offerings made of various materials, especially seals, which betray an organized community throbbing with life and enjoying close relations with foreign lands. The many Cycladic idols found together with items of jewelery and a great deal of obsidian go to highlight not only the settlement's links with the Cyclades but also the number of temporary, if not permanent, indigenous Cyc-

ladic people in the area. The scarabs, a First Dynasty vase, and seals with an early hieroglyphic script confirm links with Egypt, while a Syrian cylinder-seal, together with the extravagant use of ivory evident in the finds, constitutes undisputable testimony for relations with the East and especially Syria. Finally, necklace beads found in Tholos Tomb C so resemble those found with the Treasure of Priam at Troy as to suggest not only links with that city but also a possible answer to Archanes' source of bronze and gold during this period.

The Old Palace Period (2000 - 1700 B.C.)

Already by the beginning of the 2nd millennium B.C., the first palaces were being built in Crete while power was now concentrated in the hands of kings. At this time, the great palatial centres developed

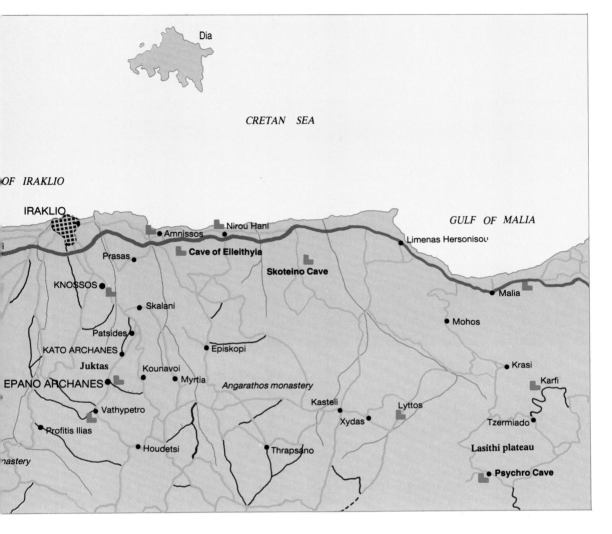

CRETAN SEA

OF IRAKLIO

GULF OF MALIA

Dia

IRAKLIO

Amnissos • Nirou Hani

Cave of Eileithyia

Limenas Hersonisou

Prasas •

Skoteino Cave

KNOSSOS •

Skalani •

Malia •

Patsides •

Mohos •

KATO ARCHANES •

Episkopi •

Juktas

Kounavoi •

Krasi •

EPANO ARCHANES •

Myrtia •

Karfi

Angarathos monastery

Vathypetro •

Kasteli •

Lyttos •

Tzermiado •

Profitis Ilias •

Xydas •

Lasithi plateau

nastery

Houdetsi •

Thrapsano •

Psychro Cave •

2. Map of the northern section of the Prefecture of Herakleion. Located at a small distance from the main city are the archaeological sites of Knossos, Archanes, Vathypetro to the south, Tylissos to the west, and Malia to the east.

the form maintained by the later (or New) palaces, a sign that they were controlled by a powerful hierarchy. Art now reached a high level of achievement testified by the utensils found in the palaces, the polychrome Kamares ware, and the fashioning of semi- precious stones. Finally there is the development of a hieroglyphic script, an indispensable tool in the dealings of those bold sailors who now traversed the Aegean.

At Archanes, vestiges of inhabitation found beneath buildings of the Neopalatial period revealed wonderful specimens of Middle Minoan (henceforth MM) IB to MM IIIA pottery (Tourkoyeitonia, the Reservoir, the Theatre area, the Vorna and Agora sites, the Papadaki bakery site, and the Kassotaki and Psaltaki plots). Important examples of Kamares ware were also found at Troullos in the vicinity of the palace. Remnants of the MM period found in the town are now more numerous, confirming that

the EM «islands» constitute part of a larger integrated settlement.

The wider area around Archanes provided more evidence of MM inhabitation. The so-called shrine in the building complex at Vitsila west of Mt. Iouktas belongs to the MM II period while further to the north, at the Kakoskalo site, an older building with a cistern can be found. MM pottery found on the Karydaki site betrays the existence of a homestead, as do similar sherds found on the Homatolakkos site east of Archanes. Furthermore, a *pithos*, or large storage jar, and MM III pottery were found at the Stravomyti cave.

3. View of Iouktas from the west.

Of greater importance are the shrines of the period. A peak sanctuary was founded at Psili Korfi on Mt. Iouktas while the possible remains of another such sanctuary exist at Houdetsi east of Archanes. However, the most significant, and for many reasons unique, religious structure from the end of this period is the isolated shrine at Anemospilia on the north slope of Iouktas. In the west room of this shrine, traces of human sacrifice were found, more on which will be said below. The destruction of the shrine at Anemospilia in 1700 B.C. by earthquake and fire coincided with that of the old palaces.

Archanes' zenith during this period is especially apparent from the cemeteries, and most particularly that at Phourni. The use of the important Tholos Tomb B continued, and towards the end of the period the tumulus known as Building 20 was built. The labyrinthine MM Funerary Building 18, which is preserved to a substantial height, revealed rich burials in *pithoi* and sarcophagi (or *larnakes*). Six burials with grave goods of pottery and seals were found in a rich cave-like grave from the MM II period on the Katsoprinia site north-west of the town.

The Neopalatial Period (1700-1400 B.C.)

After the earthquake of 1700 B.C., the palaces were rebuilt, although another earthquake occurred around 1600 B.C., possibly in connection with the great volcanic eruption on the island of Thera (Santorini). Immediately after this period, the palaces were once again rebuilt, and perhaps the ensuing age is their most flourishing prior to the final catastrophe of ca. 1450 B.C.

This was a period of general reconstruction which witnessed the development of the final form of the entire state system on Crete. With a strong fleet maintaining the Minoan «thalassocracy» in the Aegean, the Minoan miracle was accomplished by peaceful relations, not only amongst the kings within Crete, where the *Pax Minoica* held sway, but also with foreign lands. There is no doubt as to the peaceful commercial relations enjoyed between ruling sovereigns of Egypt and the East with Crete at this time.

Not only palaces, but villages and villas were also built, thus reflecting the refinement of the administrative system. Roads and harbours were constructed and irrigation and drainage systems perfected. The needs of the theocracy, with its powerful hierarchy and complex rituals, demanded large buildings with open courtyards, multiple doorways, throne rooms, dining chambers, crypts and lightwells, workshops and so on. While hieroglyphic characters continued to be employed (as in the Phaistos Disc), they began to become more stylized, eventually developing into a linear script known as Linear A.

Traces of all the elements of this unique flowering have been found throughout the excavated parts of the palace building at Archanes, and, indeed, are reflected in sites related to the settlement around the palatial centre such as at Troullos to the east and Sambei and Synoikismos to the west.

During this period, important settlements or isolated homesteads sprung up in the area around Archanes, amongst which were the thriving communities at Vitsila and Karnari to the west, the houses at Karydaki and Myristis to the north, Homatolakkos to the east, Xeri Kara to the southeast, and Vathypetro to the south. These significant settlements represented the first stage of administrative decentralization with local governors controlling production directed towards the palace centre which was responsible for the distribution or trade of goods. The road leading to southern Crete, which passes close to Archanes, is dated to the Neopalatial period.

The visible part of the splendid palace building belongs to this period. The earthquake of 1450 B.C., which levelled the whole of Crete, brought a glorious, but not the last, page in Archanes' history to an end. Contrary to past opinion which believed that only Knossos was rebuilt after the catastrophe, the most recent excavations indicate that Archanes continued to exist after 1450 B.C. Traces of Palace Style pottery are clearly apparent in the palace, but can also be found in the peak sanctuary at Psili Korfi on Iouktas, at Homatolakkos, and also at the Stravomyti cave where cult practices continued. The cemetery at Phourni also provides indications of Archanes' acme. Tholos Tomb B with its wall-painted hypostyle chamber (in which a gold ring was found) continued to be used for burials and veneration of royal personages, while the profane Building 4 in the cemetery, equipped with a wine-press and a loom, is a clear indication of the organization maintained for the care and veneration of the dead.

4. *Topographical map of the wider Archanes area.*

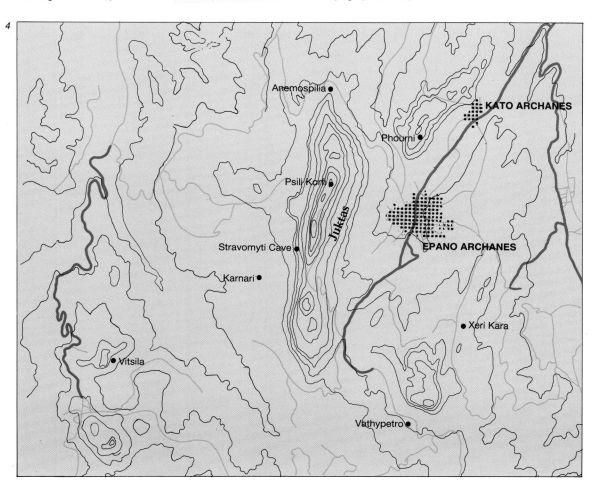

The Postpalatial Period (1400-1100 B.C.)

The coming of the Achaeans, or Mycenaeans, with their Linear B script and their more austere civilization is clearly discernible at Archanes, both in the cemetery and in the palace. The latter was indeed a very plush building and perhaps should be identified with the seat of a powerful king, such as Idomeneus who took part in the Trojan War. Plenty of evidence is furnished for a flourishing community: the palace's architectural remains, the vast amount of pottery (especially of the high-stemmed broad-mouthed goblets known as *kylikes*), the sherds at Vitsila, the cult practices at the Stravomyti cave, the goddess from «the Small Cave of Metochi», the burials at Aniforos, Mesambela, Karnari and Limnes, but in particular finds from Tholos Tombs A and D at Phourni with their plentiful jewelery made of gold, ivory and semi-precious stones, not to mention the Mycenaean Grave Enclosure. It is not impossible that Mycenaean Archanes should be identified with the Lykastos of the *Iliad* (II 647) or that Lykastos was to be found in the settlement's hinterland.

This period was brought to an end by an enormous natural catastrophe accompanied by the appearance of the «Peoples of the Sea» in the eastern Mediterranean, a time which saw the rise of another race and the final destruction of the palatial centres. A new age had dawned.

Sub-Minoan and Protogeometric Period (1100-900 B.C.)

This period is associated with the arrival in Crete of the Dorians who brought with them the use of iron and imposed demographic and racial changes on the island. A distinctive feature of this period is the introduction of cremation practices and interment of the deceased's ashes in crematory urns; a stone example was found on the Kato Lakkos site at Archanes together with an iron and bronze spear. One of the most beautiful specimens of artistic innovation from Archanes during this period is an effigy now in the Yiamalaki Collection which was found on the Fythies site north of the palace and east of Phourni.

The Geometric and Orientalizing Periods (900-650 B.C.)

Those areas settled by the Dorians during these periods witnessed the rise of city-states on the militaristic Spartan model. However, Archanes continued to thrive during Geometric times.

The baetyl found at the Stravomyti cave is proof that cult practices continued there, while important cemeteries were uncovered at the sites of Kastro, Krya Vrysi, Vromonero, Aghios Vlassis and Aghios Syllas. Fine remnants of the Geometric settlement at Archanes were found in the centre of town and on the site of the Minoan palace while Geometric sherds came to light east of Building 4 at Phourni. The long Orientalizing period (long at least as far as the arts are concerned) is represented both at the attested sites of Iouktas, Vitsila and Karydaki, as well as in the centre of the town (the Acropoli site) where important finds from the period were uncovered.

The Archaic Period (650-500 B.C.)

The Archaic period is of exceptional importance in Crete. The city-states were exclusively organized on the military model while the state system was aristocratic and conservative. Iouktas continued to be a place of worship. Art was dominated by the «Daedalic» style apparent in the Archanes area and elsewhere. From the Myristis site comes an architectural member with an *anthemion* and tendril motif from some building of the last years of the Archaic period, while fine pottery and plastic works in clay come from the centre of town; an important Archaic funerary *stele* was found in Kounavi. How ever, the wars which broke out between the Cretan cities resulted in a general decline in the quality of art works.

The Classical Period (500-330 B.C.)

The Classical period in Crete bears no relation to that in the rest of Greece. The island remained neutral during the Persian War while the squabbles amongst the Cretan city-states continued unabated. It is from an Argive inscription from this period that we find the first mention of the name Archanes, as well as of the cult practices on Iouktas. Classical sherds have been found around the centre as well as at the sites of Syllamos, Kounavi (where the «shrine of the Thracian Horseman» was located), Aghios Syllas, Karydaki and Helona. A doric column capital uncovered at the Troullos site in the town suggests the existence of an important building, and a gold cut-out found on the acropolis hints at a certain degree of affluence.

The cities of Raukos, Eltyna and Skyllous sprang up around Archanes.

The Hellenistic and Roman Periods (330 B.C. - A.D. 323)

In the Hellenistic period (330-67 B.C.) Crete

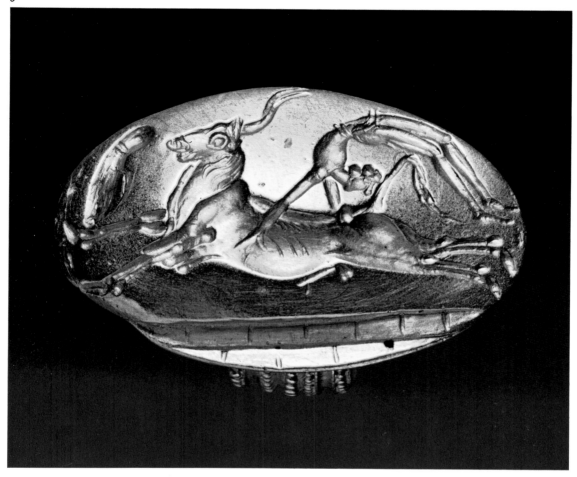

passed through a period of decline as a result of wars and the interventions of foreign powers in her internal affairs, a situation made unavoidable by alliances and treaties with the Hellenistic kingdoms of the East and Egypt. Art was now predominantly of a provincial character.

After the island's conquest by Mettelus (67 B.C.), Crete became a Roman province. Archanes is now simply referred to as a part of Knossos (*Oppido Cnosso* in the ancient texts) and was confirmed as such in an inscription of the emperor Domitian (A.D. 81-96) found at Karnari in which the boundaries of Knossos were established at that site. Roman remains were uncovered both in the wider area - at Phourni and Iouktas - and in the centre of town such as on the Ryaki site where remnants of Roman houses and graves were found. The identification of the name Archanes with Knossos during the Roman period permits the hypothesis that at least some Roman references to Knossos may in fact also refer to the city's hinterland, namely to Archanes.

5. Gold ring with a depiction of a bull-jumping scene. This was bought by Sir Arthur Evans in Archanes and in all likelihood came from a robbed tomb at Phourni. (Oxford, Ashmolean Museum).

The Byzantine Period and After

During the first Byzantine period (A.D. 323-824), Crete was part of the Eastern Roman empire up till the Arab conquest (A.D. 824-961). During both these periods Archanes followed the fate of the rest of Crete. Coins of the Arab occupation have been found in the excavations at Tourkoyeitonia. One of these, indeed, is from the reign of the emir Shu'ayb b. ab Hafs Umar, the «Saipes» of the Byzantine chronicles, son of the island's conqueror Abū Hafs Umar and ruler of Crete during the reign of the emperor Michael III (A.D. 842-867). Byzantine pottery of this period was found at Phourni. With the liberation of Crete from the Arabs by Nikephoros Phokas in A.D. 961, the fort or Rokka was built by

6. Vathypetro. View of the excavations.

Nikephoros himself opposite Vitsila. The second Byzantine period lasted from A.D. 961 to 1204 during which time Alexios I Komnenos in the 12th century dispatched colonists to occupy grants of land given to them, and Chandax (Herakleion) was elevated to the rank of Metropolitan see for the whole of Crete.

In 1204, the Byzantine state was dismembered by the Fourth Crusade and, from 1212 to 1669, Crete was occupied by the Venetians. The Morozini fountain at Archanes, together with the aqueduct and church at Karydaki, belong to this period; and Venetian coins have been found at Phourni and Xeri Kara. It was at this time that the search began for the legendary tomb of Zeus at Archanes. In a contract dated 1271, the name Archanes reappears in the historical record for the first time since the 5th-century B.C. inscription from Argos mentioned below. The church of the Archangel Michael (the *Asomatos*, or Incorporeal) was built in the 14th century with wall-paintings dated to 1315/6, the oldest examples of the Byzantine Palaeologan style in Crete. The depiction of Christ in a Frankish suit of armour is a typical product of the cross-cultural trends of the period. The modern churches of Aghia Paraskevi and Aghia Triada confirm the existence of a flourishing community.

The occupation of Crete by the Turks (1669-1898) has left its traces at Archanes, which became one of the seats of Ottoman officials even though the Sultan had awarded the then-village as a fief to Andrea Barozzi for his services in the capture of Chandax.

Today Archanes is an important economic centre.

PRESENT-DAY ARCHANES – THE SITE

Archanes, a country-town belonging to the district of Temenos in the Prefecture of Herakleion (Iraklio), is built on a relatively small, enclosed inland valley some 15 km. from Knossos with which it is linked by a tarmac road. A modern road also joins

7. Vathypetro. The wine-press.

Archanes with the settlement of Vathypetro to the south. The town constitutes the southern-most boundary of the fertile Herakleion area.

The main modern settlement, named Epano (or Upper) Archanes to distinguish it from Kato (or Lower) Archanes 1 km. to the north, lies at an altitude of 380m. in an enclosed basin surrounded by low and high hills. To the west rises the town's landmark, Mt. Iouktas (811m. high and 3.5 km. long) whose mass falls away sharply to the west thus cutting off any communication with the east. Towards the Archanes side, however, the mountain is more viable. A winding tarmac road leads up to Iouktas ending at the church of Christ the Lord (*tou Affendi tou Christou*) on one of the southern peaks.

Various roads link Archanes to Skalani to the north, Kounavi to the east, Karnari and Kanli Kastelli to the south-west, and Aghia Eleousa, Syllamos, Aghios Vlassis, and Vasillies to the north-west. The rivulet Kairatos (now known as the Katsavas) traverses the western part of the basin and, running through a gorge between Iouktas and the hill of Phourni and then past Aghia Eirene and Knossos, issues into the sea. A southern road leads from Archanes to the Messara and Phaistos.

The present settlement of Archanes is not greatly dispersed. On the contrary it appears thickly populated, consisting of various districts (Troullos, Tourkoyeitonia, Konaki, Tzami, the acropolis etc.) These districts take up the main part of the western side and centre of the basin. Only a few *metochia* (farmsteads) have been founded in some of the more isolated areas. Outside Archanes, one encounters a few small chapels such as that of the Archangel Michael (14th century) on the Assomatos site to the south.

The Archanes basin is one of the most fertile regions in Crete. The vine is almost exclusively cultivated here on wooden stacks or *krevatines*, and consists of a choice grape known as *rozaki*. The peculiar manner in which the grapes are grown lend a uniquely picturesque visage to the area. The export of these grapes, mostly abroad, provides the inhabitants of Archanes with their main source of income.

THE ORIGIN OF THE TOPONYM

The toponym Archanes is encountered in Antiquity for the first and last time in a 5th-century B.C. inscription found at Argos in the Peloponnese referring to a treaty made between Knossos and Tylissos. The inscription mentions the worship of Archos: *TON APXON TO TEMENOS EXEN TON AXAPNAI* [Archos has the shrine in Archanes]. Thus the name appears in the feminine singular Acharna. The root arch- or ach- of the name, as with the Athenian deme of Acharnai, is Indo-european and associated with water, whence many river and lake names derive (Inachos, Acheloos, Acherousia etc.) As concerns the meaning of the name, it has been said that it is related to the word *acharnos*, a type of fish, or with the word for poplar, *acherois*, found in Homer (*Iliad* XIII 389, XVI 482). In other words, the name has been interpreted by reference to aqueous elements.

Indeed, Archanes, both now and in Antiquity, has an abundance of water. As we shall see below, in Minoan times water from the Reservoir site was transported to the north, perhaps even to Knossos. During the Venetian occupation, Morozini brought water to Herakleion from Archanes (and for this reason built the famous fountain named after him in the former). Even not so long ago, Herakleion obtained its water supply from Archanes where another Morozini fountain can be found, a little outside the village between the hill of Phourni and Mt. Iouktas.

In the 14th century, travellers mentioned Archanes in relation to the tomb of Zeus located on «Monte-Jove», namely Iouktas, the Iyttos of the Argos inscription.

It is clear that, between the 5th century B.C. and the 13th century A.D., the name Archanes had been replaced by that of Knossos, of which it had become a humble hamlet in both Hellenistic and Roman times. This is confirmed by an inscription of A.D. 84 from the reign of the emperor Domitian found at Karnari west of Iouktas. The inscription refers to the establishment of property boun daries between the colonies of Kapua (which had some possessions in the area) and of Knossos, which seems to have extended thereto.

No coins were even minted by Archanes. Instead, the coins of Knossos that have been found there only provide further proof that the settlement was for many centuries subordinated to its stronger neighbour.

THE MYTH OF THE TOMB OF ZEUS

The Worship of Zeus

In the Argos inscription referred to above, where Archanes is first mentioned in Antiquity, reference is also made to the worship of Poseidon on Iouktas (*ΠΟΣΕΙΔΑΝΙ ΤΟΙ ΕΝ ΙΥΤΤΟΙ ΤΟΝ ΚΝΟΣΙΟΝ ΙΑΡΕΑ ΘΥΕΝ*) as well as of Archos, the Machaneus, and the festival of the Hyakinthia which must have had some association with the area.

The worship of Poseidon is known in Crete at Kissamos, Axos and Raukos (a site which must have been in the vicinity of Archanes). In Archanes itself, no other epigraphical testimonies exist concerning the worship of Poseidon, although the finding of a finely wrought figure of a bearded man on Iouktas makes it possible that some male deity had been venerated there over a long period.

Poseidon is a pre-Greek deity associated with female fertility goddesses such as Mother Earth, or, in Arcadia, Demeter Erinys. Thus he has certain chthonic qualities apart from his well-known association with the sea. We can trace his worship in Crete from Mycenaean times since the name Poseidon (in the feminine) exists on Linear B tablets from Knossos. The absence of a shrine building on Iouktas perhaps indicates that worship of Poseidon took place in a *temenos* (or sacred precinct); note that the epithet *Temenites* has been found in association with Poseidon on an inscription from Mykonos.

Apart from Poseidon, however, we also learn from the Argos inscription of the shrine of Archos at Archanes, as well as of the worship of the Machaneus. Both epithets belong to Zeus; indeed, the second was still associated with the god in Pausanias' time at Tanagra, Kerkyra, Kos and elsewhere in addition to Archanes. It should be noted that the qualities of both deities (Zeus and Poseidon) are often confused, for example there exists a Zeus *Enalius* (of the Sea), and a Poseidon *Cthonius* (of the Earth). Furthermore, in the myth of the Rape of Europa Zeus transforms himself into a bull (the animal which in Greek times was associated with water and Poseidon), and thus the interconnection between some of the qualities common to both deities is confirmed. The two elements, earth and water, link both deities with the god of vegetation, Hyakinthos, who is one and the same

8. Minoan bronze figurine of an «adorant», from the Aghia Triada site.

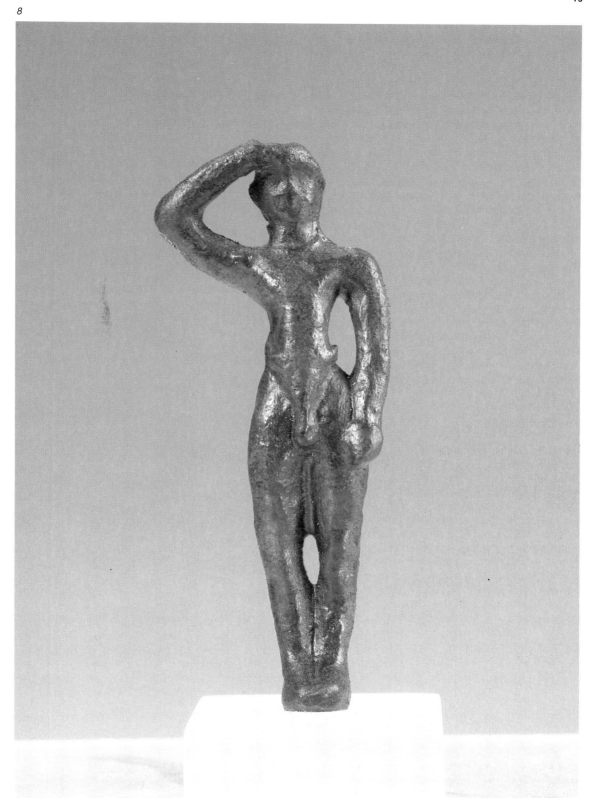

with the prehistoric god, and whose rites, the Hyakinthia, are mentioned in the Argos inscription.

The feast of Hyakinthos is nowhere attested apart from at Sparta where its origins have been traced to before the arrival of the Dorians. According to historians of Greek religion, the feast is of Cretan origin. During the festival, the so-called «grape-races» were held which have also been attributed as having some relationship with Minoan Crete, as is the lament made during the rites, which is undoubtedly connected with the death of the deity. The evidence for worship of Poseidon, Zeus, and Hyakinthos, the deities of vegetation and fertility, are exceptionally interesting, if only fragmentary. Particularly in the case of Zeus, note should be made of the discovery at Archanes of a 1st-century B.C. inscription referring to Zeus *Soter* (Zeus the Saviour), and also of the reference by Diodoros to the temple of Zeus and Hera in the «land of the Knossians», namely the wider area of Knossos. Nevertheless, the single mention in the Argos inscription of the Hyakinthia, which must be linked to the rites surrounding the deity's death, is reminiscent of the later tradition of the tomb of Zeus at Archanes, even though both were not associated from Antiquity up to modern times.

The Tomb of Zeus

Information on the tomb of Zeus at Archanes is perhaps not altogether plentiful but it is markedly persistent, especially from the later years of Antiquity. Various literary testimonies for the existence of the tomb of *Cretagenus* (or Cretan-Born) Zeus, who is indirectly associated with the youthful Minoan god and is at one and the same time both husband and son of the great Mother goddess, are based on fragments of Epimenides of Crete, one of the Seven Sages of Antiquity. No mention is made, however, of the tomb's location in Crete.

The first reference to the tomb of Zeus is made by Callimachus in the 4th century B.C. In the 3rd century B.C., Ennius identified it for the first time as being in the vicinity of Knossos (*Oppido Cnosso*). As stated above in relation to the inscription of the emperor Domitian, this term includes Archanes. After Ennius, Varro and Cicero (2nd-1st century B.C.) mention that the tomb of Zeus was one of the island's attractions. Diodorus Siculus (1st century B.C.) locates it once again in the «vicinity of Knossos» together with a certain temple to Zeus and Hera.

From the 1st to the 5th century A.D., information on the tomb of Zeus abounds. More specifically, it is mentioned by Lucian (2nd century A.D.), Por-

phyrius (3rd century A.D.) and Caesarius, brother of St. Gregory of Nazianzus (4th century A.D.). References to the tomb of Zeus appear to be constant in later Antiquity. Perhaps this is due to the writers' interest in confirming the death of the ancient god so that they might base their own theological views on firmer ground. The most famous mention of the tomb of Zeus was made by St. Paul the Apostle who with the phrase «Cretans always lie» referred to the information from Antiquity concerning the death of the immortal god.

References cease between the 5th century A.D. up to the 11th century, probably due to the persecutions of the pagans by the emperor Theodosius and the later Arab occupation. In the 11th century, the tomb of Zeus is mentioned once again, this time by the Byzantine philosopher Michael Psellos. Up till that time, the tomb is described as having been a burial mound, a monument, or simply a marker. In Venetian times, when interest in Antiquity was rekindled, information on the tomb of Zeus multiplied; now it is firmly placed at Archanes. In the 15th century, and for the first time, Archanes and Iouktas are specifically mentioned as the site of Zeus' burial by Buondelmonti. In the map prepared by his contemporary Martelli, a circular building is depicted at Archanes (but not necessarily at Iouktas) and is named by the cartographer *Sepulcrum Jovis*. In the 16th century, Barozzi refers to the tomb, which he places near Archanes.

In the 17th century and thereafter, the vicinity of Archanes and its mountain, Iouktas, is mentioned by the travellers R. Pocock, Boschini and others, not only for its natural wealth but also in relation to the tomb of Zeus. Savary, in 1779, mentioned that he had been shown the tomb of Zeus four leagues south of Knossos. These modern travellers mention the tomb as a cave, a simple grave, or a pile of stones.

In the 19th century, the travellers De Bocage, Sieber, Pashley, Spratt and others repeat information on the tomb of Zeus given them by the inhabitants of Archanes. It is possible that, from the 15th to the 19th century, information on Zeus' tomb at Archanes may in fact refer to the cemetery at Phourni, given that Tholos Tomb A, which gave the area its present name, was still visible. Thus one should not be surprised that, as we shall see below, a Venetian coin was found in that very tomb.

9. Protogeometric clay group from the Fythies site. In the middle, the goddess with upraised hands and on the roof two adorants and a dog.

HISTORY OF ARCHAEOLOGICAL INVESTIGATIONS AT ARCHANES

As we saw above, Archanes had attracted the attention of travellers seeking the tomb of Zeus at least from the 15th century A.D. onwards. Archaeological interest in the area, however, began to manifest itself only at the beginning of the 20th century. The discovery of the famous Archanes ladle in the vicinity of Troullos constituted the beginning of a series of quests for an important ancient centre in the area.

S. Xanthoudidis was the first to note the importance of Archanes in 1912, but it was Sir Arthur Evans who for the first time discerned the palatial character of the ruins. This experienced specialist in Minoan civilization, who seems to have frequently visited the site, purchased in the village the gold signet-ring with a bull-leaping scene, together with a few of the finest seal-stones in his collection, now housed in the Ashmolean Museum in Oxford.

Evans had, furthermore, noticed various walls in the village below the present settlement; some, indeed, were completely visible on the roads. More important, however, was Evans' discovery in 1922 – during building work – of the structure which he successively named the «Spring Chamber», the «Well House» and the «Reservoir.» The remainder of the last building was uncovered by J. Sakellarakis in 1964, and will be discussed below.

The data above led Evans, following typical Victorian concepts of his day, to formulate for the first time the theory that a Summer Palace for the kings of Knossos was located at Archanes. This hypothesis was accepted by S. Marinatos and N. Platon who made cuttings in the village, the former during the excavation of the megaron at Vathypetro and the latter during the course of excavations for the erection of a building. But in neither case did the sites investigated locate remains of a palace. Up to 1964 and the excavations at Archanes undertaken by J. Sakellarakis, the designation «Summer Palace» seemed nothing more than an exaggeration.

In the years since then, however, Archanes has proved to be nothing less than one of the most important archaeological sites in Crete. The collection of data from the scattered objects previously found in the vicinity of Archanes, whether now abroad or in the Herakleion Museum, as well as from the various chance finds made by locals, led to the organization of a wide-scale topographical survey. Consequently, the trial trenches opened at Tourkoyeitonia in 1964 represented the first successful excavations at Archanes, uncovering as they did the long-sought palace site. Furthermore, the discovery of the cemetery at Phourni in 1965 opened up new horizons for research.

From 1966, the excavations at Archanes have been part of the activities of the Greek Archaeological Society and continue under the supervision of John Sakellarakis and Efi Sapouna-Sakellaraki. The discovery alone of the unique Minoan shrine at Anemospilia underlines the archaeological importance of Archanes which has now become one of the most important areas for the study of Cretan history. Here one can follow the island's history from the Sub- Neolithic period right up to the modern age by examining not only domestic buildings, but cemeteries and shrines as well.

10. Clay model of a riding goddess, from the small Metochi cave.

THE PALACE CENTRE

THE WIDER AREA OF ARCHANES

Efforts by archaeologists in the past to locate the palace brought to light some information concerning the settlement, and its eastern section, Troullos, in particular. Recent systematic study has provided more complete information and thus a reconstruction of the area at not a few locations can be made.

We now know that Archanes was surrounded by smaller villages or isolated smaller centres. The settlement spread over much the same area as that occupied by the present town while the central building was equal in size to the palaces of other areas. From the eastern-most fringes of the village (the Troullos site) to the western-most (the Aghia Triada site on the eastern slopes of Iouktas) the settlement flourished during prehistoric times from the Early Minoan to the Mycenaean period, while life continued during Hellenistic, Roman and Byzantine times, and then under the Ottomans. In relation to the city which surrounded the palace, the Troullos site is worthy of mention. This site is located on the eastern-most and highest point of the hill above Archanes and to the left of the road leading from Archanes to Aghies Paraskies. Found here was the translucent alabaster ladle with a Linear A inscription, now known as the Archanes ladle. This object must date from the MM III - LM IA period (ca. 1700-1600 B.C.) Evans, in his discussion of the object in the context of the architectural remains around the find spot, believed that this was the point from which the ritual procession up to Mt. Iouktas commenced, a fact confirmed by the discovery of many similar utensils at the peak sanctuary.

Investigations undertaken at Troullos by S. Marinatos, but more importantly by J. and E. Sakellarakis, uncovered buildings of the MM II and III and LM I phases, namely from about 1800 to 1500 B.C. The architecture of the Troullos buildings is most graceful with fine ashlar curtain walls forming recesses on the outside, clay-brick partition walls on the upper floors, paved courtyards and wall-paintings on plaster. In one section discovered during the later excavations, an LM I house was discovered with five rooms, a storage room, a small courtyard and a light-well.

The movable finds from the Troullos site were likewise many and interesting, including exquisite examples of polychrome Kamares ware, vases with barbotine decoration or relief flowers similar to those found at Anemospilia, bell-shaped objects, and anthropomorphic and zoomorphic terracotta figurines belonging the Old Palace period. Also uncovered were ritual vessels, tripod offering tables, stone vases and beak-spouted jugs. A few of these vessels were also being used in the following LM I period since found with them were Floral Style ware with ripple decoration.

Both the architectural remains and the movable finds uncovered at Troullos suggest the existence here of an exceptionally important part of the settlement, perhaps an extension of the palace building or even a «small palace», thus justifying Evans conclusions regarding the ladle.

Apart from Troullos, however, not a few other sites in the immediate vicinity of the town indicate that the prehistoric settlement spread out in all directions. On the town's western fringes, at the Synoikismos site, and near the chapel of Aghia Triada (now Aghios Nektarios), a terracotta bull figurine was found along with a bronze statuette and LM I pottery. On the neighbouring Sanbei site, the head of a bull figurine was found indicating that the area was being used in the Neopalatial period. At Aghios Ioannis, where a Youth Centre is currently situated, a milk jug and black-glazed cups were uncovered from the MM I period. At the Kleidi site in the same area another zoomorphic head was discovered. At the Potamos site on the town's northern fringes, Minoan pottery and a handsome black marble pestle were found. The Lakkos site to the south of the town revealed a bronze bull figurine and a bronze chisel.

The cemeteries of the immediate area are likewise scattered. To the north-west, graves exist at Katsoprinias, to the north-east at Aniforos, to the east at Kavalaropetra, while sporadic burials from the Mycenaean period have been located at Ontades to the east and at Mesambela to the southwest. Phourni is the predominant cemetery to the north. The Hosto Nero and Stravomyti caves, and the shrines on Psili Korfi and Anemospilia are located on neighbouring Mt. Iouktas.

Apart from the city which surrounded the palatial centre, villages also existed in the wider area around Archanes. To the west of Iouktas, more specifically at Aghios Syllas, Evans noted finding MM pottery as well as figurines, whorls and loom weights which belonged to some house of the MM - LM I period. At Karnari on the Kamberi Armi site, J. Sakellarakis discovered notable Minoan pithoi. But remains of Minoan houses underneath later Mycenaean, Geometric and Archaic buildings have also been noted close to the spring. At Kato Vrysi, Geometric remains were found, while at Kastro, there is evidence for LM, Geometric, Archaic and Roman occupation. The Mycenaean burials excavated by Efi Sakellaraki, in particular those on the Tragomantra site, together with the Mycenaean pottery from the same area, highlight the importance of the site during this period.

The most important site, however, west of Iouktas is Vitsila, 2 km. from the present Kanli Kasteli (Profitis Ilias), which both Taramelli and Evans had noted. Marinatos later made small cuttings there while more recently the site was investigated by J. and E. Sakellarakis. At Vitsila, the settlement extended for about four- and-a-half-acres: it had a sturdy MM and LM wall with a *propylon* to the south; there was also an MM «Pillar Shrine» with a «Sanctuary House» made of hewn blocks, a drainage duct and a stairway. Important finds were uncovered all over the site.

Traces of a settlement were found to the north and north-west of Archanes, at the Karydaki site near the Kairatos river which flows towards Knossos and its port, Katsambas. These included a potter's wheel, a MM jug and a lamp. The finds collected from the Myristis site north-west of Archanes included, apart from a fine stone throne without a backrest, an axe and pottery from various periods. On the Kakoskalo site, MM pottery was found while MM III - LM I pottery was recovered from the cave of Aghios Antonios. These remains support the conclusion that important settlements must have existed in the area as they had further to the north at Syllamos where a pottery workshop was found.

To the east of the palace centre of Archanes and beyond Troullos, the Homatolakkos site is worthy

11. *Marine Style amphora (accurate graphic reconstruction).*

of attention. Here an extensive settlement must have flourished, perhaps similar to that at Vitsila, of which important structural and pottery remains have survived. The loom weights, the potter's wheel (corresponding to that from neighbouring Kavalaropetra), the stone vessel fragments, and the superb examples of LM I pottery found there give an idea of the importance of this settlement unit.

The Loumata site south of Archanes revealed a bronze double- axe and a dagger with a triangular blade. At Limnes, a settlement flourished during Mycenaean times. Extensive remains of an LM I

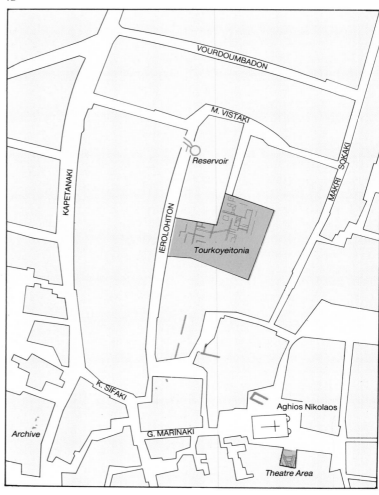

12

12. The central part of the town of Archanes with the sites where traces of the palace complex were found.

13. View of part of the excavations of the palace at the Tourkoyeitonia site.

settlement were found at Xeri Kara to the south-east of the town. The walls of certain buildings here are constructed of ashlar masonry bearing an axe-shaped mason's mark. A room with a light- well and columns was discovered, while another had a bench; a cistern and crypt were also found. Some 200m. away, other walls recently came to light. The finding of partly-worked semi-precious materials, such as rock crystal, suggests the existence of some kind of workshop. A road led from Xeri Kara to Vathypetro.

The Minoan villa at Vathypetro is located on the Piso Livadia site some four km. south of Archanes and was excavated by S. Marinatos. It seems to have been the residence of some local governor and has all the characteristics of a «small palace» with its central and western courtyard, a small tripartite shrine, a three-column stoa (or arcade), and a storeroom. It seems that the building was never finished. The upper floor apartments were used as living quarters while the lower floor was re-served for storage. Certain objects found on the lower floor such as a gold earring and a figurine were initially thought to have been found in their original position, but it is more likely that they fell from above. A wine-press in the south wing repre-sents an important find; also, an olive-press existed in the courtyard. A passage some 30m. long led to a ceramic workshop and kiln, unfortunately in a poor state of preservation today.

THE ROADS FROM ARCHANES TO KNOSSOS AND SOUTHERN CRETE

Evans traced the ancient roads of Crete in those of his own day, which followed the same course.

A road passed close by to Archanes a little further

13

up from the Venetian aqueduct at Karydaki to the north. Traces of this road were preserved at Aghios Vlassis. It followed the bank of the rivulet and after passing Karydaki continued around the north-west side of Iouktas. Thence it branched off towards Iouktas, passing Anemospilia. The road to the west of Anemospilia led in a zig-zag formation to the peak sanctuary. From Anemospilia another road led to present-day Archanes.

The main road, following the lowest point of the mountain, turned towards Vitsila after Aghios Vlassis and Aghios Syllas, passing between Iouktas and the small hill to the west known as *Mikro Iouktaki* (or Small Iouktas).

Evans also saw traces of a road at Aghia Anna which he described as between 3.80 to 4.30m. wide and resting on massive terrace walls. This is the road which joined Knossos with Phaistos and southern Crete.

Smaller roads were noted between Archanes and Iouktas, Xeri Kara, and Vathypetro. The organization and interconnection of various settlement units around the palatial centre, which served the socio-economic needs of the central unit, is thus clear.

DESCRIPTION OF THE PALACE BUILDING

The continual occupation of the town of Archanes for many centuries does not permit a complete appreciation of the palace building, which lies just below the modern houses.

Four of the sites studied within the town, however, revealed evidence for a building of palatial character:

a) The area of Tourkoyeitonia which constituted the core of the Minoan centre.

b) The area of the Reservoir next to Tourkoyeitonia to the north- west, which is covered by a house built in the 1920's and by Ierolochiton St.

c) A part of the so-called Theatre Area, and

d) The Archive area, which likewise is no longer visible today.

These four areas, of which the first two are located under a modern block of buildings and the latter two under building blocks south of the first, are the only areas of the palace which have been excavated to any great degree, and for this reason will be discussed extensively below. In the southern part of the building, however, many minor soundings made prior to modern construction works brought much complementary information to light, including evidence for older chronological periods as well. Thus EM remains were found on the Vorna site in the direct proximity of Tourkoyeitonia. After excavations had uncovered Geometric and Mycenaean levels with significant finds under Graeco-Roman buildings on the acropolis site, in the square just south of the Tourkoyeitonia building block, a Minoan layer with objects worthy of the central building were discovered. Remains of Minoan walls once noted by Evans were still visible a few years ago in the above mentioned square before it was leveled. Sturdy Minoan walls up to a height of even 2m. are still preserved in the ground floors of the houses on the eastern part of Ierolochiton St.

Further south still, close to the acropolis and on the Agora site (Arnaoutaki Pharmacy), a room was found with ashlar walls, floors covered with pebble and dash and with stone slabs, and coloured plaster on the walls. LM I Floral Style pottery was found here. That occupation continued during the Mycenaean period was evinced by figurines and high-stemmed kylikes; and even later periods were attested since 5th and 4th century-B.C. red-glazed sherds and figurines were also found.

The above sites are directly associated with the central part of the palace but, unfortunately, they were covered by modern buildings prior to the commencement of systematic excavations in the 1960's.

Tourkoyeitonia

The core of the palace building is located in approximately the centre of town, very near to the circular Reservoir excavated by both Evans and Sakellarakis. One of the central entrances to this building was discovered by the latter under an open plot in 1964. The finding of the long sought-for palace in that year was the result of a study which showed that at certain places within the town (and not around its periphery where previous archaeologists had searched) there existed walls of the same orientation which converged at a point where one would expect a palace entrance, together with its incurved altars, to be situated.

As has been noted above, the town's modern structures did not allow the complete excavation of this important building complex. However, the core of the palace provided much evidence for the nature of the building, and research was gradually complemented by the excavation of other important neighbouring plots by both John Sakellarakis and Efi Sapouna-Sakellaraki.

During the excavations at Tourkoyeitonia, a detailed stratigraphical study was made which provided important information for all the historical periods of the area, from Minoan right up to modern times. Thus it was ascertained that the area had been continually inhabited from after the 1450 B.C. destruction through Mycenaean, Geometric, Classical, Hellenistic, Roman and Byzantine times, as well as during the Arab, Venetian and Ottoman periods. The name *Tourkoyeitonia* alone (Turkish neighbourhood) highlights the Greek character of the area at large during Ottoman times, given that this specific spot was thus named to distinguish its Turkish inhabitants from the prevailing Greeks. The more recent levels have rested on the Minoan ruins without destroying them, with the exception of certain cases where material was extracted for reuse, or when deeper foundations were laid - especially during the Mycenaean period. Thus the picture we now have of the palace building belongs to one of the last Minoan palace phases which at certain points is nothing more than a repair to the pre-existing structure.

The history of the site before the establishment of the palace is less clear. As already noted, important traces of the Prepalatial period were found at the Vorna site which lies directly to the east of Tourkoyeitonia. Thus it would seem that Archanes at this time was characterized by small «islands» of dwellings which were united in the following MM period into a central building complex; the same process observed at neighbouring Knossos. The existence of important communities in the Prepalatial period is confirmed by the organization and activity at the cemetery on the hill of Phourni.

At around 1900 B.C., all the great palaces of Crete were erected. The complex at Archanes must also have been built at this time since its general conception appears compatible with this period. In

14

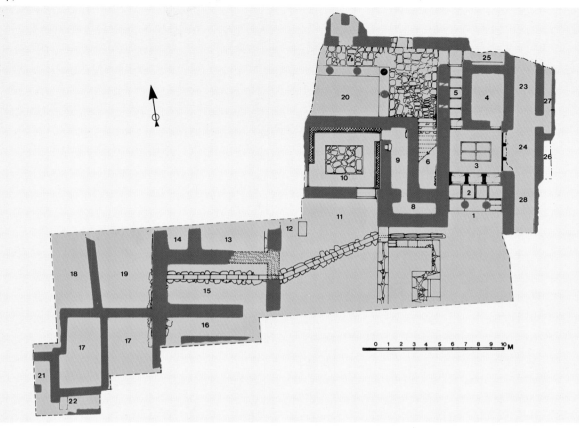

the later phases, only minor architectural changes were undertaken. From cuttings made in the building at various points (Areas 1, 17, 18), the existence of the old palace phase was determined, a phase which appears to have been rich not only at the Phourni cemetery but also in the settlement (Troullos, for example).

The size of the palace complex in its entirety must have covered the heart of the present-day town, while the Minoan settlement extended to its furthermost fringes. The extent is so great as to vindicate Evans' initial theory of a palace here. On the other hand, a question must be posed: is it possible for a second palace to be located only 10 km. away from Knossos? It should be remembered that the close distances between large centres is not unusual in the Bronze Age. Take, for example, the distance between Mycenae and Tiryns on the Greek mainland, or between Phaistos and Aghia Triada in Minoan Crete. Of course, at some stage the character of each of these twin centres should be clarified since it is senseless, as far as Crete is concerned, to stick to Evans' Victorian notion of a «Summer Palace». Such close palatial centres may have been homes

14. Ground plan of the part of the palace building on the Tourkoyeitonia site.

for important members of the royal family entrusted with various, but specific, duties and powers.

In the case of Archanes, the occupant of the palatial centre would not only have controlled the area's rich hinterland but would also have supervised the intense religious life of this part of Crete. Archanes, with its abundant supply of water (which until only recently supplied Knossos) together with the natural wealth of the surrounding area warrants the existence of a palatial centre, especially when combined with important ritual practices such as those at the Anemospilia shrine and the peak sanctuary on Iouktas. The satellite settlement-villages around Archanes, a typical example of which is the megaron at Vathypetro, confirm the need for an administrative centre in the area.

But it is not size alone which supports Archanes' palatial credentials. The very architecture of the building, the use of materials and the structural methods employed are likewise indicators of a palace complex. Elements of construction in the palace at Archanes can only be compared with those used at Knossos and Phaistos; and in no way with the provincial Malia nor, more specifically, with Zakros. A characteristic attribute, as we shall see below, is that the building has both the orientation and the piecemeal sections found only at Knossos and Phaistos (theatre area, archive room and shrines). Many types of stone were used in construction: poros-stone (the main material), conglomerate stone, gypsum, schist of various hues (blue, red), and marble (white, red, black and grey with white veins). The walls, which at some points are preserved up to 2m., are very thick so as to support a great weight. They are 0.60 - 0.70m. wide, except for the outer walls which are thicker than 1m. The length of some of the poros-stone blocks is greater than 2m. and many bear mason's marks, usually tridents or double axes. These elements, together with the quality of the finds, leave no doubt as to the building's nature.

At Tourkoyeitonia, the part of the complex accessible to visitors is located between Ierolochiton St., whence the present approach, and a long narrow street known as Makri Sokaki. On entering the site the visitor first encounters Area 21; however, it is preferable to begin the itinerary at one of the more easterly entrances north of the courtyard.

At the eastern part of **Courtyard 1**, which extends westwards (Area 11) and is divided in the middle by a platform, the visitor can see a large pile of fallen stones left undisturbed from the final destruction of the palace which give a graphic idea of the terrible catastrophe wrought by earthquake and fire. Cuttings made at the north-west part of this courtyard uncovered traces of the earlier palace. Bell-shaped objects and figurines found from this phase highlight the sanctity of the area both in the older and the later palatial periods.

At Antechamber 2 just to the north of the courtyard, one can see the remains of the imposing **entrance** the sides of which consist of large ashlar blocks of exceptional quality. The threshold is constructed of three large plaques also made of hewn poros-stone. The existence of two columns which once supported the first floor is attested by two

15. Reconstruction of part of the south facade of the palace building on the Tourkoyeitonia site, with the altars and the «Platform».

16. View of Areas 1-5 of the palace building from the south. Above the threshold are the marble column bases and to the right the incurved altars.

marble bases dressed with plaster and wedged into openings in the threshold. Part of the wood used for these columns was preserved during the excavations, and thus their precise diametre can be calculated. It is certain that the upper stories, whose architectural elements came crashing down into the courtyard, were equally as elaborate as those of the ground floor.

The passage between the eastern column and its neighbouring anta was closed up with four incurved altars set on the threshold, each of which measured 0.35m. high and 0.48 x 0.48m. wide. When joined together they formed an altar (0.96 x. 096m.) Here, for the first time in the Cretan-Mycenaean world, do we find incurved altars in such an arrangement even though this type of altar is known from depic-

tions on seal-stones, where they are usually shown with branches laid upon them. The most famous parallel example is that in the relief depiction on the Lion Gate at Mycenae where the two beasts tread on just such an altar while flanking the central column resting upon it. Various interpretations have been given as to the meaning of this depiction, but it is now almost certain that the arrangement of the incurved altars is associated with some «sacred gate». Just south of the altars, a porphyrite lamp and white marble slabs with black veins were found; no doubt fallen from the upper floor of that section of the building east of the open Area 1.

The entrance opens up to the north into **Antechamber 2**. The antechamber's floor was decorated with a series of coloured stucco squares between which some perishable material was once laid. Wall-paintings, now much destroyed, no doubt adorned the entire wall-surface. Only on the east wall did the excavations find visible traces of a wall-painting, in this case depicting a woman, possibly a priestess, holding a branch – a well-known motif from the Cretan-Mycenaean iconographic repertoire. She wears a dress with frills and has her hair elaborately gathered and with long curls.

The antechamber enters Area 3 by way of a multiple doorway, or *polytheron*, with three openings whose base of fine gypsum is now discernable by its whitish colour. **Area 3** is exceptionally spacious and by means of another multiple doorway, likewise with three openings, it communicates to the east with the ground-floor Areas 24 and 26. From the area's north-west corner, Corridor 5 leads to the north and east apartments. A doorway in the northeast corner leads to Room 4.

Area 3 is square. Its floor is lined with a red plaster skirting around the edges and even at the openings. A square with an inscribed cross, also of red plaster, decorates the floor in the centre of the room. The inside squares formed by the cross arms would have been dressed with reeds or wood, while the section between the walls, the openings and the central square were covered with a pebble floor. The walls here were also covered with a fine layer of plaster, perhaps decorated with wall-paintings. Thus this main part of the entrance would have been exceptionally impressive with its varied trimmings and decoration.

Found in the middle of Area 3 was building material fallen from the upper storey, together with 43 loom weights and ten whorls made from semi-precious stones, an indication that the upper floors of this section of the palace were also of some importance.

One must imagine Area 3 not only as a venue for people to congregate in front of Room 4, but also as facilitating movement through the multiple doorways to the other areas opening off therefrom. As already noted, the eastern multiple doorway led to the ground floor areas below Areas 23, 24, 26 and 27. Excavation of these areas is still underway and the ground floor has not yet been discovered.

The surface of the second storey excavated up till now indicates that **Areas 23 and 24** consisted of a long corridor on a certain floor, which possibly terminated at the northern anta of the multiple doorway.

A wall built of fine poros-stone blocks with trident mason's marks exists between Areas 24 and 26, the highest extant wall in this section of the building. The gypsum antae still visible on huge plaques, together with their transverse arrangement in relation to the walls, betray the presence of a multiple doorway on this floor as well. The contents of these floors will be recovered in future excavations of the ground-floor areas. However, various unworked stone fragments found hereabouts may point to a stone-cutter's workshop in one of the upper stories.

At the point where Areas 23 and 24 diverge, **Corridor 27** opens to the east and veers northwards. South of this is **Area 26**. The narrow Corridor 27 was found full of marble plaques which undoubtedly had fallen from the upper level. Together with the white lime plaster which covered all the walls of these east apartments, these plaques clearly underscore the refined construction and luxury of the rooms. The abundance of stones found therein shows that the upper storey was also built with stones. Perhaps the walls of the stories even further up were made of mud brick.

Room 4 is perhaps the most important part in this section of the palace. The architectural development here clearly suggests an integrated conception and confirms the view that all the details were planned at the same time. A characteristic indication of this can be found in the precise alignment of the central square in Area 3 with the axis precisely between the two columns of the Antechamber and that of the central opening of the southern multiple doorway, or polytheron. To the north, the central square of Area 3 looks onto the wall of Room 4 flanked by its entrance and the opening of Corridor 5 going north. Note that the architectural planning, and consequently the function of this blind Room 4, is suggested by the fact that its only entrance is off centre; and indeed on the axis of the incurved altars at the entrance.

Room 4 was also at least two-storied. The second storey, which was slightly smaller judging from the sockets in the west and south wall, was divided into two parts: one to the south and one to the north. Piles of bricks found in the north-west corner of the ground floor indicate that they were possibly used in the construction of part of the floor's superstructure, or even of a storey higher up. A column stood in the centre of the upper storey between the northern and southern sections; its stone base was found where it fell, high in the fill of the floor below. The floor of this upper storey was paved. Bands of red plaster were found here, suggesting that the fringes of the walls, at least of the north section, were skirted in the same manner as those in the ground-floor Areas 2-3.

The ground-floor level of Room 4 is also significant since it remained undisturbed after the destruction of the palace. Its sturdy walls were covered with a fine layer of plaster, no doubt decorated

with paintings. Severe damage marked the lower part of the west wall. The plaster here had fallen away from a point below a straight line along the wall, thus suggesting that the decoration terminated at this line. Most probably, the lower part of the wall was adorned with some perishable material.

Plaster must also have covered the floor, at least at its centre. The western wall had a low bench made of stones dressed with gypsum and no doubt used to support objects. A somewhat higher fixture of *kouskoura* stone characterized the north wall in the north-west corner, while the north-east corner was furnished with a stepped platform perfectly aligned with the axis of the doorway and the incurved altars. The platform was constructed of kouskoura slabs, mud bricks and wood, covered by

successive coats of fine plaster and then coloured or decorated. Both here and in the north-west corner, pronounced traces of a powerful conflagration are apparent, no doubt due to the falling wooden pillars supporting the upper floor but also to the burning of the wooden wall-dressing, and perhaps that of other free-standing object or objects.

The central ground-floor level of Room 4, invisible from the doorway, was found badly burnt, possibly proof that some wooden object or fixture had stood there in a position corresponding, perhaps, to the column on the upper floor. To the right and left of this spot were found two large and heavily decorated ritual jars, one decorated with spirals and the other with finely fashioned palmettes and other foliate motifs. The lid of the second jar was found nearby decorated with clumps and crocuses. Also found were a host of smaller vases and many other objects made of precious materials (ivory, a large piece of red jasper etc.) Room 4 is thus immensely significant not only for its construction and preservation, but also for its finds.

The wide **Corridor 5** heads north from the west of Room 4. The corridor's east wall is solid, but the western has an opening, perhaps from an older

17. Clay vase from Area 4 decorated on the body with palms, vines and other plant motifs, and with crocuses on the lid.

18. Ornate stone lamps – of porphyrite – heavily decorated with spirals and leaf motifs. From Area 25.

18

phase, at its north-west anta while one or two other openings appear some way higher up. The corridor's floors are also decorated with bands of red plaster forming squares while the walls were dressed with plaster and, in all likelihood, adorned with frescoes.

Corridor 5 is closed off to the north by a wall. However, two doors at this point open to the east and west respectively. The eastern door leads to **Area 25** the northern section of which has not been investigated as it lies under a modern building. Nevertheless, the small southern section which was excavated brought important finds to light. On a bench dressed with gypsum plaques running along the south wall, two exceptional specimens of Minoan stone work were found: two lamps made of porphyrite. One of them is decorated with a relief spiral, while the second bears delicately executed foliate motifs. A peculiar clay vessel was found in one of the lamps. Under the bench, a jar was found, which had evidently fallen from above. Uncovered

a little to the north was a vase with beautiful lily decoration which seems to have been ready for use.

The burnt frame of a wooden doorway found in the east wall indicated that ascent to the first floor was made from the east.

The west door of Corridor 5 leads to a large right-angled space consisting of the gamma shaped Stoa 7 to the north-east, and Light-well 20 at the south-west corner. At this point, the picture presented by the conflagration is unique: the earthquake and accompanying fires destroyed the palace at many points to such an extent that reconstruction was not possible in the years after the final collapse. This is certainly the case here. The gradual image presented by the excavations is of a catastrophe of biblical proportions. Huge square blocks of poros-stone or ironstone, often measuring 1.75 x 1m. and 0.50m. wide, were found in successive layers with thick clay-earth (which once covered the walls), bricks from the partition walls, and burnt wooden

columns, dressings and lintels. The stones have in most cases been completely crushed, and in others (such as the gypsum blocks) have been pulverised so completely as to constitute with the clay a crust so thick as to make even the identification of individual structural elements difficult.

Areas 7a to the north and **7b** to the east constitute a large, spacious ground-floor stoa that meets a stairway leading to the upper floors at its southeast corner. To the north, and in the same well-built wall going east and blocking Corridor 5, a large doorway has been opened with windows further to the west: holes on the wall by the windows suggest that they were latticed. Two long rooms going north to south at the north-west have not yet been excavated, but may have constituted a small stairway.

Nevertheless, the significant width and position of Stoa 7's north doorway indicates that the main approach to the upper floors was made from the large staircase 6, 8, and 9 to the north, more on which

19. Reconstruction of Light-well 20 and Stairway 6 as they would have appeared from Areas 7a and 7b.

will be said below; the magnitude of the building is thus further suggested.

The gamma shaped **Stoa 7** was paved with green and red schist plaques surrounded by red and yellow bands of plaster. In the corner of the right-angle, the ground-floor colonnade is visible, as are the fallen walls of the upper floors. The stoa was supported by columns. The bases of the columns of the ground floor were found buried under the material from the second and third floors. The colonnade of the upper floor was similar to that of the ground floor, with the exception of the pillar which replaced the corner column employed on the ground floor. The floors of the upper stories, which must have numbered at least three, were also paved with blue and red schist plaques.

The floor of **Light-well 20**, the area enclosed by

the corner of the colonnade, was laid with blue and red plaster too badly burnt now to discern any possible decoration.

Areas 7 and 20 were used as passage-ways and for lighting and few finds were thus recovered from therein. Unlike the other finds, the many clay loom weights which fell into Area 7b suggest that industrial installations existed in some of the rooms of the upper floors of this section.

As we have already noted, Stoa 7 was used as a passage way for the ascent to the upper floors via the large staircase in Areas 6, 8, and 9. Area 6 was the first eastern leg of the stairway going from north to south. Area 8 represents the landing, and Area 9 the western leg going from south and north: the very same arrangement and orientation as that of the famous Grand Staircase at Knossos. The eastern leg – **Area 6** – was constructed on a strong base of kouskoura while the lower steps were dressed with schist plaques. The edges of the steps, west and east, were lined with red plaster bands which lent a pleasing aspect to the structure. From **Landing 8**, which had a tower-like outer appearance, windows overlooked the central Courtyard 1 and the «Platform» with the altars. Window-frames from at least two stories were found in the courtyard and it would seem that the building's occupants looked down on activity in the courtyard below from these very windows.

Areas 8 and 9 on the ground floor would have been ancillary areas for Hall 10. Just at the south anta of the opening from **Area 9** to Hall 10, a vat-like structure with clay walls was preserved to a height of 1m. The stone plaque with a pronounced depression, which constitutes the vat's floor, was covered with a host of upturned plain conical cups, a clear indication of ritual activity at the moment of destruction. The floor depression continues underneath the eastern wall of Hall 10 where it is then lost into the earth, once again confirmation of cult use of the area.

From Courtyard 11 access can be made to **Hall 10**, a significant room which certainly had a second, if not a third, floor. The contents of the second floor are known together with the fact that, unlike the ground floor, it was divided into two by a transverse wall going east to west. The religious function of the northern of these two rooms is proved beyond doubt by its contents, which fell to the ground below where they were found. These include a large stone sacrificial altar, measuring 1.66 x 0.55m. by 0.19m. high (now situated in Courtyard 11 in front of Hall 10), about 30 tripodal plaster offering tables,

and two horns of consecration, likewise of plaster. Further proof from the ground-floor deposit for a shrine on this floor is provided by a poros-stone base with an incision for a double-axe. Many pot sherds and other objects lay nearby, together with bull and other zoomorphic figurines, and part of a black steatite lamp. Animal bones, possibly the remnants of sacrifices, were found slightly above the floor of the bottom storey. Plaques of veined marble suggest that the upper floor was paved, while the walls would have been lined with red plaster. Traces of the fire which calcined everything are abundantly clear.

The ground-floor Hall 10 had another door in the south-west corner leading west to an area now under private land, and thus not available for exca-

20. *Reconstruction of Room 10 with the bench, from the south. A triton and stone vase were found here.*

vation. A window-opening in the south wall of Hall 10 bears holes for a lattice cover. Along the west, north, and east walls, benches had been built and then dressed with gypsum plaques which were subsequently calcined during the conflagration: their bases were decorated with bands of plaster. The centre of the room was paved with a rectangular blue marble floor with coloured plaster pointing and skirting. A raised dais in the centre of the north wall, 0.60m. high and made of hard stucco, may have supported a seat made of perishable material. A depression and channel in the floor next to the dais would have had some ritual use.

A unique jug-like vase made of veined marble found in the centre of the room was found to contain a triton shell. The use of this mollusk shell in invoking the deity is confirmed from a depiction on a well-known seal from the Idaean Cave. A bronze chisel and a marble pestle for the admixture of certain solids was found together with a large number of other significant objects.

Hall 10 thus constitutes one of the most important areas in the palace, constructed as it is with expensive materials and provided with important ritual vessels throughout both its floors.

Courtyard 11 consists of the continuation of Courtyard 1, which is divided by the «Platform» mentioned below. Its fill gave up much material

21. Horns of Consecration and a tripod plaster altar fallen from the upper floor into Room 10.

from the upper stories of Areas 10, 8, and 12. Large ashlar blocks from the windows, finely-worked poros blocks with mason's marks from the outer walls, and other building materials are typical of the finds in this area. A drain crosses the courtyard diagonally from north-east to south-west and continues to Area 15. The drain, 0.28-0.39m. wide and 0.28m. high, was lined with poros-stone slabs and may have been similarly covered, as certain points of Area 15 seem to indicate.

As mentioned above, Courtyard 1/11 is separated by the «**Platform**» located just in front of the tower-like construction of Area 8. Characteristically, its width is the same as that of the tower and it likewise continues in a southerly direction; it has not, however, been fully excavated as yet. The «Platform's» strict assimilation to the palace's architectural plan not only indicates that it is contemporaneous to the building, but also highlights the integrated organisation of both interior and exterior areas, a factor perhaps not unrelated to the activities inside and outside the building.

The «Platform» is a rectangular construction of hewn poros- stone blocks, and may have had a low balustrade dividing it from both sides of the courtyard. This interpretation is supported by the mass of poros-stone blocks found both left and right but especially by the hinge-pin socket made for a door in the north- west corner of the threshold. At the south-east corner of the «Platform» is a paved area which may have been the site of the poros-stone pyramidal double-axe base found a little to the west. The rest of the area was covered with soil, perhaps used for the cultivation of some plant or tree associated with cult practices.

The entire length of the «Platform's» northern extent is taken up by tall, broad, rectangular poros-stone altar dressed with slabs of the same material. This type of altar had not been actually encountered up till now, although it was known from iconographical reproductions. Attached to the western end of the trapezoidal altar is a small poros-stone construction resembling a stepped altar, a type that is attested both in the iconographical and the archaeological record: for example, that found at Anemospilia and elsewhere.

Constructed between the facade of the palace and the altars was a small narrow stone drain that must have played some role in those rituals conducted at the altars and on the «Platform». Note that this drain leads from the north-east corner of the trapezoidal altar, follows its northern edge and spills into the drain of Courtyard 11 underneath the threshold of the doorway.

Apart from the animal bones found on the «Platform» and a triton shell similar to that found in Hall 10, part of a stone libation table and a fragment of a stone vase also came to light here, along with about 40 plain conical cups which, together with the double-axe base mentioned above, delineate the ritual use of the area and, indeed, the offering of libations.

The north-west corner of Courtyard 11 was termed **Area 12** to distinguish it from Hall 10 and Area 13 in regard to its building material and the objects fallen from above which were uncovered here, which included fragments of a poros-stone Horns of Consecration. The terracotta zoomorphic figurines and a seated human figure also found here associate the location with Area 13 and with other finds that fell into Courtyard 11 from Hall 10. It thus seems possible that the terrible force of the earthquake hurled objects from another specialized area into the courtyard. On the other hand, it is not im-

possible that the large stone block at the south-west corner of Area 12 is in fact a type of altar and that some of the objects mentioned above did, in fact, fall from it.

Of the adjoining and spacious **Area 13** only the south part was excavated since private land occupies the site to the north. Once more, objects fallen from the upper floor were uncovered here: slabs of white, red, blue and green marble that, although of varying size, would have formed a rectangle when joined together. Thus the room above Area 13 would also have been luxuriously constructed. The many brick fragments found here show that they must have belonged to some internal partition wall on the upper floor. On the ground floor of Area 13, over 100 vases were found, including 40 amphorae, cooking pots, and conical or globular cups. The quantity of amphorae and cups may indicate the existence of a storage area or a venue for feasts.

22. View of Courtyard 1-11 with the «Platform», the altar and the drain.

22

The narrow **Area 14** to the west of Area 13, which extended northwards, gave up no moveable finds. However, the floor surfaces of the upper stories are interesting in that they are constructed of a type of mosaic (pebble and dash) found both here and in the fill of Area 19.

Area 15 is an elongated open-air precinct constituting an extension of Courtyard 11 to the south of Areas 13 and 14. The large drain dissecting Courtyard 11 is continued here, spilling out into Area 19. Its extension was evidently made of clay. At one point, the drain preserves its original covering slab. Together with Areas 21 and 22, Area 15 is one of the few areas where Mycenaean walls have been preserved, while Mycenaean occupation in the vicinity manifests itself only in pottery and a thick layer of stones. As in Areas 1, 11, 16 and 17, many Mycenaean kylikes were found here.

South of Area 15 lies **Area 16** which is entered by a wide doorway whose hinge was found in situ. Area 16 is long and narrow and was evidently two-storied since finds (once again fallen from above) included Horns of Consecration, fine pieces of delicate pottery and cups, and a piece of gold leaf. These last finds associate Area 16 with the adjoining Areas 17 and 17a. It thus seems possible that none of the upper floors in this area had an industrial function, even though a mortar was discovered. The area was adorned with coloured plaster. An opening at the south-west corner leads to apartments further south which have not yet been excavated.

The eastern section of the palace building terminates at this point with a sturdy pseudo-isodomic ashlar wall running north to south and dividing Areas 14, 15 and 16. In Areas 17-21 to the west, the architecture is completely different. The walls here are constructed with smaller and badly hewn stones closely resembling the architecture of MM tombs at Phourni. However, the ashlar blocks found here which had fallen from above confirm that stone of more refined workmanship was employed in the upper stories. Consequently, it is possible that at this point in the hill-slope the builders of the new palace used as a base those walls of the old palace which had not been destroyed. The sturdy wall running from north to south is associated architecturally with those walls of the western section, resting as it does on top of them. The drain from Areas 11 and 15 disappears below this wall.

Area 17a, which has yet to be fully excavated, is directly associated with Area 17 to the west in relation both to the pebble and dash floors of the upper

stories and to the coloured plaster. Marine Style pottery was found here along with pieces of ivory, a shell-shaped steatite amulet, and so on. However, the spherical loom weights found here firmly associate Area 17a with the upper stories of Area 19. A circular hearth or altar constructed of small stones (0.95m. diameter) and located at a higher level may belong to the Mycenaean phase of the palace, as does a faience bead found amongst the stones used in construction.

The gamma shaped **Area 17** (named the «Shrine of the Ivory Idols») is one of the most important areas of the palace since each of its floor levels, that must have numbered at least three during the Neopalatial period, provided exceptional and significant finds. Construction of the bottom floors used walls of the old palace, while standard ashlar blocks were employed for the upper stories. Many fragments of coloured plaster were found at various levels, and although much destroyed, they still betray the radiance of the original colours. It should be noted that no traces exist for a doorway to this room, despite the considerable height (2m.) of the extant walls.

The southern-most part of Area 17 was partly destroyed by the deep foundations made for a Mycenaean building. These Mycenaean ruins together with those of Area 15 are the only later structural interventions to have survived. The fine Mycenaean kylikes found in adjoining areas were also encountered here in abundance and indicate the area's importance even after the final destruction of the Minoan palace.

The upper stories seem to have been residential quarters, unlike Areas 18 and 19 which were industrial, since only fragmentary finds were made of loom weights and conical cups. Perhaps a loom existed in one of the upper floors, or possibly some of the floors were allocated as women's quarters given that one ivory and two bronze pins and a silver earring had fallen thence, to be found in a lower level to the south. The stratigraphical confusion of material from both the upper and the lower floors resulting from the catastrophe is highlighted by the mixture of floor materials from both stories. A transverse partition wall fallen from above, and now in

23. View of part of the excavations on the Tourkoyeitonia site, from the east. The «Platform» and the drain are visible.

the centre of the area, testifies to the differentiation of room areas in one of the upper stories.

Immediately below one floor surface, which was well water- proofed with a material known by locals as *lepida* (flakes or chippings of soft stone), a room was discovered which once must have been adorned with fine wall-paintings if the bright plaster fragments of red, blue, and orange are anything to go by. Significant finds here helped determine the area's nature: a tripodal plaster altar, part of a steatite altar, a mortar, 40 vases and the braided head of a terracotta anthropomorphic figurine.

Two interesting poros-stone pyramidal double-axe bases were found aligned on the room's north-south axis. A group of fruit- bowels and a stone *pyxis* were found around the northern base; to the west was a clay tray with the skull of an animal, and to the east, a stone altar with animal bones in the hollowed centre of the upper surface. The southern base was only fragmentarily preserved but was also surrounded by significant finds: two animal skulls, and a bull figurine. It is not certain whether these two bases were exactly in this position just prior to the catastrophe, but it is quite possible that they belonged to a large area above the ground floor of Area 17, and perhaps to Areas 21 and 22. This is most likely since a collection of interesting objects of a uniform character was found between them. More specifically: a wonderful group of Marine Style vases comprising a set of various shapes, many of which had similar decoration (octopi, sea anemones, argonauts etc.) The most important find, however, made between the two bases was a chryselephantine group consisting of at least six figures. In Area 17, two ivory heads were found as well as three feet and a hand, all of varying sizes; there were also pieces of gold and silver leaf, and an ivory fish. In the adjoining Area 22, an ivory arm was discovered belonging to a lost figure with upraised hands, together with a miniature foot which undoubtedly belonged to the same group. This would indicate that the objects were hurled from above during the earthquake. The pebbles and a few shells found with the ivory fragments – and which certainly fell with them – suggest that we have here a ritual group that may be in some way associated with the aqueous qualities of the deity worshiped here. It is no coincidence that Marine Style vases should have been found at this very spot.

Other finds only go to support the area's religious use: an intact triton together with a piece of lapis lazuli, and a rhyton; while a conch in the south wall containing upturned cups is reminiscent of the «cupboards» attested in ritual ceremonies. Furthermore, a white marble pommel found here must have belonged to a ritual rod or dagger.

The picture of a lavishly decked out area is complemented by the finding of an ornate stone altar adorned with torsional relief foliate motifs. Two seals found in the western part of the room, one with a depiction of a female figure and the other showing a wild goat, are certainly associated with the silver earring and the three pins mentioned above. It should be noted that older excavations at a point corresponding to the south of Area 17 (and now under the modern road) uncovered an ivory pyxis and part of a stone lamp, a bowl, a stone altar and a double-edged dagger which belonged to two important areas that must have been contemporary with and adjacent to Area 17; they may, in fact, even belong to the same group.

Religious use of this area in older periods is borne out by the recovery from the MM III - LM IA levels of animal skulls accompanied by trays, bell-shaped figurines, three stone vases, a terracotta relief with spirals, a communion goblet like that of an earlier type found at Anemospilia, and more particularly of a heart-shaped ladle similar to that uncovered at Troullos. The great amount of pottery is also closely related to the contents of the later phase. Thus Area 17, apart from the wealth of its finds, undoubtedly represents an area with especially pronounced religious functions throughout all its Minoan and Mycenaean phases.

Area 18 must have been located on the side of the hill, as were Areas 17 and 19. Areas 18 and 19 were covered with enormous amounts of accumulated fill due to the incline of the hill. Thus at certain places Minoan levels are uncovered at a depth of 1.80 to 2.00m. Later interventions, however, in particular the «German trench» going south to north dug at a great depth during the Occupation, brought pottery and other finds from the Minoan period to light.

Area 18 is located on the north-west corner of the excavated area. Its north and west side, and perhaps part of its east, have not been uncovered; neither has any passage or doorway been found that communicates with other areas. The highest stories of this area should be associated with Area 19 as study of the fill bore out.

Associated with the until now western-most area of the excavation is a wall which was first excavated in 1965 and is now located underneath Ierolochiton St. This may have constituted the western-most boundary of Area 18 or some other area further to the west. A potter's wheel found there may provide a link between this locality and the industrial activity on the upper stories of Area 19. The Marine and Floral Style pottery together with a series of other finds links it to both Areas 17 and 19.

The *lepidochoma*, water-resistant earth used in the roof and various types of floor surface and found in fragments between ash layers of burnt wood, testifies to the exceptional care shown in the construction and decoration of Area 18, the walls of which were coated with a thin layer of polychrome plaster with red the predominant colour. Fragments of a plaster relief depiction, possibly representing two female figures in blue attire on a white ground, exemplify the variety of ornamentation used here.

These finds may represent the contents of an area located above both Areas 18 and 19. Worthy of mention are censers, vases with Floral Style decoration (sacral-ivy, leaf, and lily motifs), a few Marine Style wares, a triton, a bird's nest vase as well as part of an ornate porphyrite conical rhyton.

Like other areas, so this one rested on the ruins of the 1600 B.C. destruction level. A thick layer of pottery from this period was found underneath the wall which divides Area 18 from Area 19. Here, at least, the arrangement of the new palace does not seem to have followed that of the old.

The northern-most part of the adjacent **Area 19** has likewise not been excavated. The fill here was deep; and a door, if there was one, has once again eluded discovery. This is a spacious area which seems, however, to have been divided into smaller areas over various stories. Area 19 also underwent intense burning, so much so that it is now difficult to attribute finds to specific locations. It would appear that certain industrial areas are represented in the upper levels, especially in the southern-most part, since a number of loom-weights and three piles of conical cups were found therein, together with pigmentary materials (red, blue and yellow), mortars and pestles, and shells and obsidian blades. If the finds and the structural nature of the building are a reliable indicator, the utilization of other floors or of adjoining areas of the same floor as that of Area 19's final phase was perhaps different. The walls were covered with polychrome plaster (blue, red, orange) adorned with miniature depictions of marinescapes, animal and vegetal motifs such as ivy and reeds against a red ground, and even plastic affixes such as relief shells and hearts. The roof was made water-resistant by the appli-

cation of lepidochoma while the floors were paved with schist slabs, various types of pebble and dash, as well as marble slabs with polychrome stucco pointing. Slabs of local kouskoura were used here for shelving where space permitted. The eastern wall was built of poros-stone, a fallen block of which bears a trident mason's mark.

Significant movable finds were found here. A gold cut-out was discovered in a conical cup, and the horn of an animal in another; definitely suggestions of ritual use and certainly not everyday custom. Bull, goat, and braided anthropomorphic figurines also betray cult practices.

More objects seem to belong to older MM IIIA and LM IA levels which show pronounced traces of destruction by fire: a bell-shaped figurine and barbotine ware, stepped cups and pottery with light-on-dark decoration. The area was exceptionally important at this stage, and may have had two-storied buildings contiguous on its neighbouring areas, especially Areas 17 and 18.

The powerful destruction apparent here both in LM IA and LM IB, not to mention later disturbances, do not permit the archaeologist to reconstruct a detailed plan of the rooms. The different consistencies in the lepidochoma used in the roof and those of the pebble and dash floors do indicate, however, that many repairs were made, perhaps even within the same period.

Areas 21 and **22** to the west and south of Area 17 have not yet been completely investigated, although work continues. Both underwent wide-scale interventions during the Mycenaean and later periods, with the Mycenaean intervention destroying many of the upper Minoan deposits due to very low foundation walls. Area 21 and Area 22 preserve remains of the Mycenaean building which utilised material (chiefly ashlar blocks) from the Minoan palace. This Mycenaean building had given up wonderful examples of LM IIIA- B pottery.

Area 21 is a narrow area with elements suggesting a staircase. Area 22 is likewise elongated and communicates with Area 21, but also has access to the southern-most apartments by way of a door in

24, 25. Two plastic ivory heads from Area 17, one of a youth and the other of a mature male. Together with the ivory limbs, hands and feet, and with a wooden core, these constituted a group of at least six chryselephantine figures. ►

its south wall. A large rectangular plaque on the western-most part of the area may have served as a threshold for the ground or first floor.

Objects similar to those uncovered in Area 17 were also found here, such as terracotta figurines, two parts from the ivory group of Area 17 (the upraised arm and the miniature foot mentioned above), a seal-stone depicting a lion, a clay object with an incised depiction of a Gorgon-like creature, and important Marine and Floral Style pottery also belonging to the group found in Area 17.

The Reservoir

In 1922, Evans located part of a circular underground poros- stone Reservoir which may originally have been vaulted (dimensions: 2m. long, 0.60m. wide, 5.45m. in diameter, and about 6m. high), and aligned with Area 18 to the north. The part of the structure Evans found was fully excavated by J. Sakellarakis in 1964. Its floor was laid with pebbles and 5 steps led from the north to the water level. The circular structure, in effect, surrounds a spring.

Today, the Reservoir is partly covered up by Ierolochiton St. and partly by houses which had already been built in 1964.

Water from the Reservoir passed over a stone, found to the north-west side, which was placed at the head of the conduit: this stone had a depression turning into a channel which fed water to the conduit. Thence, the drain, made of poros-stone blocks 1m. wide by 1m. deep, travels westwards. The whole system is reminiscent of the Great Drain of the Ancient Agora at Athens while, from the point of view of construction, it resembles that at Mavrokolymbos at Knossos.

As is the case with Zakros, the Reservoir is located within the palace area. It seems to have been built during the Old Palace period and destroyed in LM IA. In LM IB it was reused after repairs had been undertaken. Much Floral but less Marine Style pottery was found around the drain and in the vicinity.

In the period of the New Palaces, a verandah seems to have existed to the west. A large number of flower-pots were uncovered to the south of this structure and must have originated from some balcony in the palace building since their find context included traces of red plaster similar to that discovered in the apartments of the same building. The great amount of flower-pots points not only to the beautification of the Reservoir area but also to rituals involved in the worship of water, for also found here were bell-shaped objects and zoomorphic

figurines from the palace's oldest phase. Figurines from a later period were also discovered.

With the final destruction of the Minoan palace, the Reservoir fell into disuse and collapsed. A human skull bears eloquent and rare testimony (together with the remains from Anemospilia) to the loss of life occasioned by the catastrophe, probably as a result of falling masonry. In Mycenaean times, the area seems to have continued in use although it is not clear whether the Reservoir still supplied water or whether another building was simply erected on top of it. It goes without saying that this Reservoir is important for our knowledge of Early Minoan mechanical and hydraulic systems.

As the Reservoir indicates, the Tourkoyeitonia building complex extended to the south and west, and other associated parts of the complex have been uncovered extending to the south, west and south-east: for example, the Theatre and the Archive Room.

The Theatre Area

The Theatre Area stands a short distance away from the palace complex to the south-east of the building's centre and south of the church of Aghios Nikolaos. This area also underwent destruction due to later Mycenaean, Greek and Roman interventions that probably had no relation to the area's original use: at one later stage, indeed, it may have been used as a workshop for ivory and semi- precious stones.

The main part of the Theatre Area was paved and dissected by four «walkways» which together form a triangle. A double walkway is located to the east, vertical to which are two separate but parallel walkways to the south running west to east. The double walkway and the southern walkway are linked by a fourth walkway with a channel running along its south-west flank. A stepped altar rests on both the fourth walkway and the paved area and would no doubt have been accompanied by the double Horns of Consecration with an incised branch, found fallen in the centre of the area. Along the length of the channel is a huge slab some 4m. long and 1.50m. wide on which plain conical cups were found.

The paved area, the altar, the channel and the large hewn blocks, not to mention the sacred Horns of Consecration, all have their parallels in the theatre areas of other palatial centres. The stepped structure is known from the Zakros rhyton and depictions on seal-stones. Finally, two examples from

26

Archanes itself – one from the palace near the elongated altar, and one from Anemospilia – together with another older one from the central court at Phaistos confirm both its use and the relationship of theatrical events with religious rites.

In 1990, the theatre's exedra (measuring 4.90 x 3.50m.) was discovered to the north-west of the church of Aghios Nikolaos.

The Archive

The continuation of the palace building was found a little further to the south-west of Tourkoyeitonia and at other points on the Tzami site, of which the Kalpadaki plot on Kapetanaki St. is especially interesting.

Here some of the most important parts of the palace were located. More specifically, Linear A tablets, one of them double- sided, were found alongside MM III - LM IA pottery.

We do not know much about the architecture of the Archive area apart from three parallel MM III - LM IA walls and a partition wall which were excavated. The face of the strong wall preserved here,

26. Reconstruction of the «Theatre Area» excavated at the Aghios Nikolaos site.

however, employed ashlar masonry, a common feature in the rest of the palace building. The doorway and the anta, as well as the polychrome plaster and the pottery, link these areas with the main complex of the MM III - LM IA period. Furthermore, traces of an LM IB destruction level were also evident underneath the Mycenaean layers.

Traces of older MM IIIA - MM IIIB phases were also discerned here. In the two rooms from this phase, walls with polychrome plaster were found. One of the rooms of the older building provided important evidence for our understanding of Minoan architecture: a model of a house, the features of which all go to complement our knowledge of the architecture at Archanes. In the same place unworked pieces of rock crystal, obsidian, and steatite were found, thus indicating that a workshop may have once been located here. Unfortunately, this significant administrative area is no longer accessible to visitors.

27. Clay Linear A tablet, from the Archive of the palace building.

MOVEABLE OBJECTS AND DECORATION

The importance of the palace complex is reflected not only from the exceptional nature of its construction, the wall-painted decoration or the evidence for multi-storied buildings, but also from the number and quality of the finds made therein.

Painted decoration

Wall-paintings constitute the first indication of luxurious ornamentation of the palace building. Even though much destroyed, the wall-paintings of Archanes nevertheless provide some wonderful examples of iconographical motifs. The walls were covered with white plaster onto which blue, red and yellow bands were painted, or, alternatively, with red or blue plaster decorated with both geometric and naturalistic motifs.

Despite the fact that the frescoes are only frag-

mentarily preserved, various types of decoration are discernible such as simple geometric motifs, comprising mostly of polychrome bands or red corners on a white ground, and undulating wavy lines. Vegetal motifs were also employed with ivy, and papyrus and reed-like plants to name a few. Marine motifs such as miniature fish and sea rocks, but mainly sea shells in relief, are other favorite themes of the Archanes painters, while depictions of humans also seem to have been popular. A section of a relief wall-painting preserves the shoulder of a woman with a thin mantle thrown over it. The badly preserved fresco in the entrance depicts a woman offering a branch to an altar. Some specimens of zoomorphic depictions are also evident, and thus it would seem that the repertoire of scenes and motifs was large.

Decorative bands of coloured stucco lent a colourful and tasteful appearance to the floors with their crosses and pointing in combination with straw mats or pebble floors. Furthermore, the sense of luxury was accentuated by different kinds of flooring material: mosaic, schist slabs, and multicoloured marble by itself or in combination with polychrome bands.

Stone architectural elements, altars and vessels

Other elements, both moveable and immoveable, complemented the fine architecture of the palace such as altars, sacred Horns of Consecration and various pedestals or bases of sacred axes.

The altars at Archanes are of a single class but of many types, a phenomenon unique in Crete both in terms of number and of variety. To begin with there is the set of four incurved altars at the entrance between Courtyard 1 and Area 3 which constitutes an exceptional group. This rare altar type is encountered elsewhere only in double arrangement in the Lion Gate relief at Mycenae.

The large elongated fixed altar south of Area 8 and on the north side of the «Platform» between open Areas 1 and 11 is also known from iconographical types, especially from depictions of animal sacrifices, although it remains unknown at other sites. This construction is especially impressive both for its size and the wealth of its detail such as the poros-stone plaques used to finish the top and the channel at its base.

Also known from iconography is the stepped structure found at Archanes next to the elongated altar. On the Zakros rhyton and a later Mycenaean

28

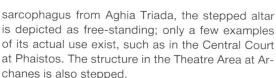

29

sarcophagus from Aghia Triada, the stepped altar is depicted as free-standing; only a few examples of its actual use exist, such as in the Central Court at Phaistos. The structure in the Theatre Area at Archanes is also stepped.

The large stone table found in Room 10 constitutes another kind of altar known from animal sacrifices. Altars of this type may have stood on wooden pedestals. The smaller and poorly fashioned altar with a central channel found in Area 17 represents a variation of the above-mentioned altar types.

These altars were constructed of poros-stone and constitute part of the architectural make up of the building complex. Poros- stone was also used in the manufacture of other items of religious use, such as Horns of Consecration (Areas 10, 11 and the Theatre Area) and bases for double-axes (Areas 10, 11, 12, 17).

Utensils made from material employed in building construction also went to give the palace at Archanes a luxurious air, for example the white portable tripodal altars made of plaster and decorated with red and blue bands. Thirty such altars were found in Areas 10 and 19.

28, 29. Fresco fragment with a plant motif and plastic plaster decoration. From the excavation of part of the palace building at the Tourkoyeitonia site.

Other ritual vessels were made of polychrome stone, such as the small stone portable altars: two steatite examples were found in Room 17, one of them close to the double-axe base. The second was tripodal, ornate and decorated with vegetal motifs. Yet another made from similar material was found on the «Platform», and a fourth was found in an extension to the palace in the centre of the modern town on the Relaki site. Similar small altars were also uncovered west of Room 21, as well as in the peak sanctuary on Psili Korfi and at Troullos.

The «ladles» also belong to the category of stone ritual utensils. The most famous is the heart-shaped specimen made of white alabaster, found in the first decade of this century at the Troullos site in an MM pottery context. Examples of a similar shape were found at Phaistos, Palaikastro and elsewhere. The Archanes example bears a carved inscription corresponding to those on a stone tripartite vessel from Psychro and a goblet from Palaikastro. The

30. Stone shell, from the Troullos site. A carved Linear A inscription appears at the lip.

script is Linear A with a total of 24 letters. Certain characters have been linked to the symbol for «sceptre» and «throne» by Evans who believed that the inscription bore some relation to the worship of the Minoan goddess, and even that a «small palace» must have existed in the vicinity of the find spot, from which the procession to Mt. Iouktas would have commenced. This theory eventually proved to be apt, although such ladles were also found both in the palace building (Room 17) and in the peak sanctuary of Psili Korfi.

Lamps, both stone and clay, constitute yet another valuable item made primarily for practical use, but with decoration that has claims to artistry. The most important of these are the two porphyrite examples found in Area 23. Both bear relief decoration: one with floral motifs of exceptional delicacy and the other with a pronounced running-spiral in relief. Both were found standing on the same

bench, and a third clay vessel was discovered inside the second.

The other stone utensils found at the Troullos site include a steatite axe made for ritual and not every day use. Small marble spool-shaped pestles - whence they often take their name - were found in the central palace building (Room 10) as well as in caves (the Stravomyti cave), and in settlements (Potamos). It seems certain that these fine objects were used in the grinding of certain substances, perhaps during the course of special rituals.

Many stone vases were also found either complete or in fragmentary form. Amongst these is an exceptionally handsome work, a so-called sauce boat of grey-blue marble with a heart-shaped handle found in the ground-floor of Room 10. In Area 18, a stone bird's nest vase was found as well as part of a porphyrite conical rhyton. Apart from the well-known ladle mentioned above, Troullos also provided two stone bird's nest vases. Furthermore, a great number of other stone vases was found in the Phourni cemetery. Quite often these vessels were accompanied by triton shells (Rooms 10, 17, 19, and the «Platform»). Only one clay triton imitation was found in a pyxis at Vorna.

Terracotta and ivory figurines

Figurines constitute yet another find category. Apart from bronze and ivory figurines discussed below, a relatively large amount of both anthropomorphic and zoomorphic terracotta examples were discovered. Bull figurines were found together with the 30 altars and the stone table from the upper floor of Room 10; a zoomorphic figurine was uncovered in contact with the elongated altar north of the «Platform», and another was found in Area 4. In Area 12, animal figurines were found together with a terracotta seated human figurine. In Area 16 more terracotta objects were discovered: two animal figurines, a pair of Horns of Consecration, a female figurine with upraised arms, and a head. The figurine of an adorant was found in Area 19, and a fine head with long braids in Area 17. Figurines were also found near the Reservoir, while bell-shaped objects (evidently imitations of ritual masks) associated with the old palace were uncovered below the floors of the new palace from Areas 17 and 19 as well as from in front of the entrance (Area 1).

At Troullos on the outer limits of the palace complex bell- shaped, anthropomorphic and zoomorphic figurines were found as well as a plastic terracotta flower from the Old Palatial period. These finds are directly related to those from Iouktas and justify Evans' opinion that the procession to that mountain started from this point. In Mycenaean years this tradition continued.

The two bull's head rhytons also found at Troullos are exceptionally important.

Unlike the terracotta idols common to peak sanctuaries and domestic shrines, ivory figurines are very few in Minoan Crete. The groups from Knossos and Palaikastro are the most important found so far. But now Archanes can also be said to constitute an important ivory centre; indeed, perhaps the most important since the tradition here began in the EM period as we know from plastic ivory seals from the cemetery at Phourni.

The figurines found in Area 17 certainly must have been *acrolithic*, namely with their main body made of some perishable material such as wood (ebony), which was burnt in the fire, but the extremities fashioned from ivory. The figurine heads are typified by their naturalistic treatment with the hands and feet distinguished by their plastic appearance. All in all, the parts collected belong to at least six figures of which the largest would have been at least 12cm. high, while the foot found in Area 22 is of minuscule size. The group must have belonged to a similar set to that found at Knossos. Together with the ivory fish, the sea shells and the pebbles, these must have constituted a «scene» that would have rested on a bench in the shrine.

The heads preserve traces of colour – in particular the larger whose head-band is rendered in red –, while apertures in the smaller example may have served to facilitate the attachment of the hair, possibly made of another material as is the case with the latest such finds from Palaikastro. The fine gold bands which were also uncovered could have served as locks of hair, while the wide gold bands and the gold and silver cut outs found with them may have rendered a loincloth, tiara or any other item of dress. In short, we have here a chryselephantine group.

Inlays of precious materials

Many other materials were used, however, by the inhabitants of this part of the palace. Semi-precious stones were combined with other materials such as faience to decorate items other than jewelery and seal-stones: for example, small chests, or games such as chess. Inlays of various shapes were found in rooms of the palace. Ivory and stone rings, of

31

31. Clay bell-shaped figurines of various sizes, from the Phourni cemetery. Fragments of similar figurines were uncovered during excavations at the Tourkoyeitonia site.

course, decorated certain wooden vessels. In Area 18, rock-crystal inserts were found. But it was Area 19 where a host of inlays were found which once adorned an important item, perhaps a chess set: plaque-like and lentoid rock-crystal, leaf- shaped obsidian, ring and disk-shaped bone and green steatite; all these contributed to what would have been a handsome piece of craftsmanship. Perhaps the inlays in Areas 17 and 18 came from this same item and, like the pottery, were scattered over different areas.

Metal figurines and utensils

Although the metal objects from the palace are few compared to those from the cemetery, nevertheless they include some truly exceptional pieces of fine quality.

The mass of obsidian found indicates that this material had not been entirely replaced by bronze as a raw material for tools and implements. However, many bronze utensils both inside and outside the palace constitute an important group together with those found at Phourni. Finds from outside the palace include double-axes from the Loumata, Vorna and Votzi sites as well as the daggers from Troullos and Loumata. A bronze handle was found in Area 10 and a double-axe for practical use was found on the surface in the vicinity of the palace, while excellent examples of weaponry were uncovered at Anemospilia and Phourni.

Many figurines and double-axes were found on Iouktas. From the settlement area came a very significant bronze figurine as well as parts of an idol from Area 1. A zoomorphic figurine was found on the Lakkos site.

The finding at Phourni of other older bronze figurines indicates that bronze-working flourished as much in the MM as in the LM period. Recent studies have even revealed the existence of an important local workshop. A figurine now in the Benaki Museum must have come from the Archanes workshop. A small spoon found in Area 10 and the double-edged dagger from the settlement had some practical use, while two tweezers from the settlement together with a ring from Area 18 are amongst the few personal items found in the palace and the settlement. The lack of more such finds is perhaps due to the fact that the inhabitants took their precious metal utensils with them on abandoning the palace.

In the palace, the existence of lead is represented by two plaques found in Area 10. They would undoubtedly have belonged to a casket whose remaining parts were hurled to another, and as yet unexcavated, part of the palace. A lead disk weight from the Plaka site now in the Herakleion Museum is related to economic activity in the area.

Pottery

The majority of finds, however, is represented by the pottery found in abundance all over the palace and the settlement. Minoan pottery from Archanes is indeed of outstanding quality both during the earlier and later periods.

EM Vasiliki ware found in the palace and Aghios Onouphrios ware from the Stravomyti cave highlight the refined art of the EM period, while more evidence for the ornate vessels of the age came from the Phourni cemetery.

MM Kamares ware pottery, also found at Phourni, includes fine examples of this style from the period of its acme, while examples from Anemospilia trace its development during its later phase. Relief decoration, the barbotine vases, spirals, floral motifs, and countless more examples are just a few of the decorative characteristics typical of Archanes Kamares ware. One may also mention the stepped cups (which by themselves constitute the local «Archanes style»), cups with relief flowers and animals (such as the bull on the Anemospilia bucket), ornate vases with carinated rims, delicate egg-shell ware, pithoi and jars, not to mention all the household vessels which continue as pottery types into the next period with little variation: all these give a picture of prosperity and refinement during this phase.

In the Neopalatial period, pottery with floral and marine motifs reflects the naturalistic inclination of the period. The most common motifs of the Floral Style are reeds, pea vine with spirals, ligulae etc., while the Marine Style is unique both in the craftsmanship of the vessels and its decoration: octopi, sea anemones, coral and rocks predominate. The pottery types are many and varied (amphorae, jugs, conical and ovoid rhytons, jars, cups of various shapes sometimes found in whole sets with the same decoration, such as in Area 17). The inspiration of both design and rendition, the fine clay, the attractive slip, and the colour are typical of these exquisite ceramic products.

Special mention should be made of the everyday coarse ware which was often stored or piled up in small areas. Amphorae, fruit-bowls, cooking pots, censers, large and small trays, shallow bowls, and jars were found together with some of the most important vases, a fact which clearly shows that large numbers of objects from two stories used for different purposes were compounded during the collapse of the building. Flower pots constitute another category and are encountered mostly in Area 19 and the Reservoir. Conical cups represent the least important, but by far the most abundant vessel type and are found throughout the site. These had had a variety of uses ranging from ritual to domestic and industrial.

Jewelery and seal-stones

In contrast to the cemetery, only a few personal items have been found in the palace, some of which have already been mentioned. These consist mostly of seals, earrings, amulets and pins. The latter were used to clasp some item of clothing, although the more delicate specimens seem to have attached a veil to the hair. They may even have been used to fasten the hair itself, as the location of one such object in a burial in Tholos Tomb D at Phourni seems to testify.

Seals are also few in relation to those found in

32. Marine and Floral Style clay cups of various shapes decorated with argonauts, crocuses, papyri, figure-of-eight shields, double axes etc. From Area 17 of the palace building.

the cemetery. Of those found in the palace, a lentoid seal-stone depicting a running bull was found in Area 10. Two steatite specimens (one depicting a woman executing a ritual act and the other a mountain goat) were found in Area 17, while another with a griffin was uncovered in Area 19.

Beads, another personal item, were found scattered around the palace, evidently a sign of sudden and violent departure. A steatite shell-shaped pendant was found in Area 17a and an amulet of rock-crystal in the Acropolis area. In the Theatre Area, the only jewelery found was a foot-shaped amulet.

Gold objects are also few compared to the cemetery and seem mostly to have been combined with other materials, chiefly ivory.

Personal objects seem mostly to be associated with those areas characterized as shrines, although they do not appear to have been votive offerings. Perhaps they are proof that the last to abandon the palace were the priests who left behind them these mementoes of their abrupt departure.

Weaving

Finally, there are the objects associated with weaving. The spherical loom weights found in many Areas (e.g. 19) are so numerous that they must have come from a large number of looms in the same vicinity. Thus justification can be provided for identifying at least part of this area as a weaving work shop. Individual looms may have existed in other rooms where fewer weights were found – Area 17 for example.

The whorls needed for spinning were usually made of clay. They are not so numerous and are usually encountered individually both in the central and surrounding buildings. However, a group of these objects made of semi-precious materials was found in Area 3, which justly may be christened «the Chamber of the Stone Whorls». Ten whorls were found together in this Area: one of black stone with apertures for inlays, three of rock crystal, one each of steatite and other stone material, and even one of ivory. A fourth stone specimen was found in Area 4. A specific social class obviously did not deign to use common wooden or clay whorls for spinning.

On the other hand, rock crystal, steatite and ivory were used for weaving implements, as we know from objects from other parts of Crete and from Mycenae.

LIFE IN THE PALACE AND THE CITY

The description of the architectural remains of the palace and the finds made therein, together with the little but instructive information concerning the city and the wider area, allow us to reconstruct a reasonably vivid picture of life here during Minoan times.

The area of Archanes has been continuously inhabited from Neolithic times (c. 6000 B.C.). In the EM I period, the community there seems to have arrived at that stage of development we call agricultural, while data chiefly provided by the Phourni cemetery points to some kind of urban organization in the EM II period with the parallel growth of contacts with the outside world. Nevertheless, a central authority acting as a link between the various tribes still does not appear to have existed at this time.

Only in the MM period, at around 1900 B.C., do we find extended settlements organized around the central palace building. Hamlets spring up even further away; Vitsila, for example, to the west and Homatolakkos to the east. Shrines also begin to manifest themselves such as the peak sanctuary of Psili Korfi and, later, that at Anemospilia, while in the LM IA period (ca.1600 B.C.) new and important settlement units appear at Xeri Kara and Vathypetro.

These centres undoubtedly inter-communicated, and must also have maintained contacts with Knossos. Clear signs of communication are provided by the roads that were discovered running from Archanes to Iouktas, as well as those to southern and central Crete. While we disagree with Evans' theory that the Kairatos rivulet once constituted a navigable and direct link with the port at Katsamba, it is nevertheless certain that roads leading to Knossos – which existed till only recently – would have carried carts drawn by oxen, and later horses, towards the northern port. Thus life and movement between centres must have been lively, with farmers, herdsmen and merchants operating both within and outside the settlements.

The inhabitants of the area, at least those belonging to the upper class, must have enjoyed a comfortable and pleasant life style. The more humble classes, however, would not have lacked similar comforts, as the construction of the settlement's houses and the utensils found therein seem to indicate. As a consequence, gaping social divisions probably did not exist.

The Minoans, including of course the inhabitants of Archanes, thus seem to have lived in conditions of internal and external peace, a factor which must have influenced all aspects of social activity. The customs of everyday life, in as much as we can reconstruct from the remains of domestic quarters, were those of an exceptionally refined community. The number of domestic vessels would indicate that a great number of people, whether permanent or temporary residents, lived and worked in the luxurious and richly decorated buildings of the palace complex.

On the other hand, the prehistorian must take great care to avoid conjuring up false impressions of both the life style and the function of piecemeal areas of a specific settlement when interpreting its remains. Many problems are caused for the researcher by the collapse of many building stories, one atop the other, and the subsequent discovery in a single place of many objects which, in fact, originated in different areas.

It is almost universally accepted that the discovery of ritual objects in the same context as utensils or implements of everyday use must necessarily indicate the co-existence of these two different functions in a single location. This is so much so that workshop-shrines seem to be almost commonplace. Without wishing to exclude the possibility that shrines co-existed with storage areas or workshops – and those areas where no upper storey exists obviously provide a far clearer picture of the situation – it must nevertheless be stressed that such generalizations are perilous. The priest-king who oversaw the production and dissemination of material goods, in addition to supervising the religious functions of the state, is no doubt related to his «brother» king in Mesopotamia who was endowed with similar responsibilities and authority. But these two civilizations, Mesopotamia and Crete, differed in very significant ways so that an interpretation of phenomena in both areas on the same criteria is not possible.

The central building at Archanes provided sufficient material to answer various questions concerning the general atmosphere of the palace areas, the utilisation of the courtyards and industrial areas, the arrangement of some of the upper stories, and so on. Much information, moreover, is still buried in the ground.

For instance, we are still unaware as to which areas served as sleeping quarters. One hypothesis states that bedrooms in the palace were located on the upper floors so that ventilation and a pleasant view could be afforded the tired Minoan. A ready answer for the disappearance of evidence for sleeping quarters is provided by a bed made of wood and hide found preserved on Thera; namely that beds were made of perishable materials. The clay caskets in which the deceased were interned would have been useful in life as receptacles for covers and clothes, while clay tubs were used not only in the interests of cleanliness but also for the burial of the dead. Lamps would have existed in all rooms, while a few caskets made of perishable materials would have served to store valuables which the owner would undoubtedly have kept close to his person on being obliged to leave in the wake of a catastrophe. Examples of all such items were found in the areas excavated, although to pinpoint their original position within the palace is not always possible.

Our information on sanitary systems and diet are more complete. The description of the Reservoir and the drains show that watering and drainage systems were of high technological specifications, and it seems that both rain water and springs were exploited, an example of the latter being the aqueduct-Reservoir.

Of course, it is not possible to reconstruct completely the drainage systems since the clay pipes of the palace, in their present shape, are located underneath the floors. However, quite a few sections of pipe have been preserved, as well as U-shaped clay conduits. Overground channels made of stone supplied the aqueduct with water, and may also have been used for drainage: for example, those in Courtyard 11 and Area 15 which are covered with stone slabs.

In general, reservoirs served as a focal point for the life of the community where people would frequently congregate. The many pots for flowers or plants usually found at such venues must have stood on the porches or next to the rooms with their finely decorated walls. One also finds figurines from both the older and the later phases of the palace. Indeed, we may go as far as to accept Evans' hypothesis of «hanging gardens» that would have been enjoyed during leisure hours and used as venues for ritual ceremonies. A parallel example can be found in the reservoir at Zakros.

Areas for the collection and storage of agricultural products were carefully chosen in accordance with the demands of hygiene. Here both livestock and crop products were stored, although they may have been processed in the settlement units outside the palace building. At Vathypetro and elsewhere, for example, wine was made and then transported to the centre for distribution and partial consumption. Olive oil may have been produced both inside and outside the settlement since large mortars have been found, but in nowhere as great a number as the smaller mortars with which other agricultural goods were ground.

The kitchens, chiefly known from the areas excavated near the central building, were always situated on the ground-floor and furnished with circular or semi-circular hearths open at the front. A few clay partitions were used to store utensils. The mass of portable tripodal cooking pots shows that these vessels could have been used either in an open space or over an open fire. The large amount and variety of mortars and pestles for the grinding of wheat or aromatic herbs suggests that a variety of concoctions was produced.

The dining areas were very close to the kitchens, if not in the same location since shallow bowls and trays, amphorae, jugs, fruit-bowls and cups are usually found alongside the cooking pots. Hundreds of conical cups from one of the stories of Area 19 indicate that some large room served as a hall for symposia which may have been associated with populous ceremonies. While life outside the centre bears all the marks of a farming community, activity within the centre, likewise pronounced, was chiefly geared to the processing of agricultural products and raw materials that reached the palace from without.

Apart from food preparation, other operations within the palace from centre were organized on a strictly hierarchical basis, as the allocation of areas seems to indicate.

According to the finds and information provided by later Linear B inscriptions, the many and varied tasks involved in the production of fabrics were undertaken by both men and women. Shearing was mostly done by the men, while dying, spinning and weaving occupied the women. The most important natural dyes used crocuses, saffron, pomegranate, myrsine and walnuts. Also used, amongst other materials, was the blood of various insects, murex shell, indigo, mineral colours and perhaps iron oxides. A group of conical cups found mostly in Area 19 played some role in textile production (possibly as containers for dyes) since they were found with loom weights and coloured mineral sub-

stances (yellow, red, grey-blue). The abundance of weights shows that this area housed an industrial installation with many upright looms. The rock-crystal, steatite and ivory whorls found in Area 3 indicate that spinning also occupied the more refined classes. Embroidery, which we know must have existed because of the complex motifs employed on textiles depicted in frescoes, would have constituted a separate activity. Weaving, therefore, must have constituted a major industrial activity, and indeed the end product may have been exported since we know of the existence of textiles made by the Minoan *Keftiu* from Mesopotamian sources. What we do not know, however, is whether a specific class undertook the sewing of the complex garments with their fringes, complicated belts, and feathers, and the construction of masks for certain ceremonies. It is not impossible that this may have been the work of private handicrafts.

The many pieces of stone and ivory found scattered over various areas in both the palace and the domestic areas suggest that some manpower was employed for stone-cutting or miniature sculpture. The many seal-stones that have been found show that the artists at Archanes fashioned exquisite specimens of miniature stone-work, and, indeed, did not confine themselves to stone but also used ivory, as is evident from the many fine examples from the cemetery and the palace from the EM period right up to the end of the Mycenaean years. Furthermore, a special category of artist may have been entrusted with the fashioning of stone vases and lamps.

The craftsmen employed in making architectural members would undoubtedly have fallen into a third category under the supervision of the architect. They would have been joined with carpenters, plasterers and wall-painters. The miniature «Archanes house» may have served as a model to guide workers involved in building construction.

Potters would have formed another class. The

34

35

33. *Pithos from the Kamberi Armi site.*

34. *Large pithoid vase with «pea-vine» decoration. Found at the Galano Papouri site.*

35. *Clay cooking-pot from the Troullos site. Fragments of similar vessels were found during excavations at Tourkoyeitonia.*

potter's wheels found at Archanes, both in the central building and in the outlying areas such as Syllamos, Kavalaropetra, Homatolakkos etc., in association with the abundance of vases, seem to indicate that pottery was also a domestic industry. In the palace itself, the areas west of Area 18 and 21 gave up potter's wheels which suggest that here we have the site of the pottery workshop.

The site of a bronze workshop remains unknown. It must, however, be considered certain that in both the old and new palace periods, local craftsmen produced those bronze figurines found at Phourni and on Iouktas, as well as those uncovered in the outlying areas of the palace. The group of bronze figurines from Archanes is amongst the most important to have been found in Crete and must have been manufactured by more than one person at any given time, a theory given credence by the bronze vessels, tools and weapons found in peripheral areas of the palace. The workshop itself must have been located very near to the central palace building.

Mention, of course, must also be made of the goldsmiths whose delicately fashioned masterpieces were mostly found in the cemetery at Phourni. No doubt, they constituted a select class of craftsmen.

All these activities, together with their related ancillary tasks, demanded an organizational system to control production and distribution, and which hired officials charged with mediating between the local governors and the kings, under whose direct control and protection all activities came. Thus a system of inspector-clerks and supervisors developed to record orders, commercial agreements, and incoming or outgoing goods; a system similar to those we know existed in the other great civilizations of the period in Egypt and Mesopotamia. The Linear A tablets found at Archanes are eloquent proof of such a process.

Although not a coastal settlement, the inhabitants of Archanes must have included sailors and traders. These men would have brought precious materials from foreign lands, materials which we now find in various sectors of the settlement at large. Some of the *Keftiu* traders depicted in Egyptian wall-paintings bearing exotic goods (oil, wine and dittany) may have come from Archanes itself. Thus a life rich in materials and ideas can be gleaned from those areas of the settlement excavated to date.

Social life in Minoan Crete was mostly interwoven with various religious and political activities similar to those which today accompany the celebration of Saint's days or the visit of important foreign potentates. Private events such as birth, death and marriage were also natural parts of life. The needs attendant on political events, agreements between neighbouring regions, and exchanges of goods allow us to imagine the palace centre on certain days bustling with crowds drawn from peoples of various races, including dignitaries and traders from Egypt and the East bringing gifts or products for exchange, or simply observing the multifarious ceremonies. At great feasts, striking garments would have lent a festive flavour to the proceedings. The number and quality of the vessels that have been found to date show a degree of refinement enviable even by modern standards.

Religious ceremonies, moreover, would have had a particularly ritualistic nature if the distribution of vessels and the variety of cult centres is anything to go by. More particularly, Archanes has for the first time provided examples of all the types of shrine, each one throwing light on some specific devotional function which took place there. Thus we can now follow these shrines' operations through all their phases. We know that in the early period, worship took place in sacred caves in the vicinity, discovered last century at the Stravomyti and Hosto Nero caves on the south slope of Iouktas.

A second type of shrine is the «peak sanctuary» such as that uncovered by Evans at Psili Korfi on Iouktas where mostly popular festivities with bonfires took place. These festivals were attended by a host of people who gave votive offerings of animal and human limb replicas made mostly of clay, but sometimes of bronze: these resemble the *tamata* widely offered in Modern Greek churches. The festivities were accompanied by ecstatic rituals and magic dances during which the heavenly hypostasis of the deity was mostly worshiped. The «saluting» pose of most of the many figurines found at peak sanctuaries (namely the stance with one hand to the eyes to avoid the glare of the sun) is undoubtedly related to the brightness of the deity's epiphany or of her representative priestess who appeared with upraised arms or in a gesture of blessing with both palms facing downwards. She also wore a high conical tiara similar to that of the «Mountain God» known from Asia Minor. Perhaps the chthonic manifestation of the deity was also worshiped here with the deposition of votive offerings in crevices (such as the double-axes found at the Psili Korfi sanctuary), as was the supraterrestrial «Mistress of Animals» known from a sealing found at Knossos.

36

36. A unique clay model of a house.

Special ritual ceremonies involving only a few people and possibly executed «in secret» (similar to those referred to by Pausanias in later Greek times) would have taken place in the important tripartite temple at Anemospilia, whose architectural type is known from many Minoan depictions. These rituals, which may or may not have involved the shedding of blood, were performed by members of the royal family in front of the life-sized cult statue of the deity (the *xoanon*). Other rituals included «Lustral Cleansing», and the dressing of the cult statue at a special location after a procession bearing the peplos, or shroud, in precisely the same manner known from depictions on Minoan seals and from the later worship of Hera. The parallel with the famous processions of the Panathenaia and the Eleusinian mysteries is obvious. A corresponding ceremony is portrayed on the Thera frescoes where female figures prepare to dress the priestess, the terrestrial representative of the deity. Furthermore, Minoan seals and the Aghia Triada sealings depict figures carrying «sacred vestments» and the sacred knots used

in ritual ceremonies. Some form of ritual meal may have accompanied these rites, as seems to be indicated by the many vessels found at the shrines which are no different from domestic wares.

Other types of shrine within the palace complex itself had specialized functions. Although much has been said concerning those exaggerated claims which attribute most utensils found in settlements to ritual use, it should not be forgotten that even today most important civil events are inter-linked with religious festivals in both the provinces and cities (Saints' days, Feast days etc.) Thus, it should not seem at all strange that the presence of cult objects found in various places should consequently underscore the character of the period's shrines and religious beliefs, especially when we consider that magic and religion played an important part in everyday life at this time. Furthermore, religious life would no doubt have been accentuated in this so-

ciety with its prevalent theocratic system, although one should naturally not infer that religion pervaded every single aspect of everyday life.

The transferal of shrines from caves and other natural settings to man-made structures was already underway by the MM period, but was completed only during the last palace phase. Thus tripartite temples such as that at Anemospilia could now be found not only in the palace, but also in domestic buildings. These are the so-called domestic shrines which manifest themselves in a variety of types. In the vicinity of Archanes, a tripartite domestic shrine was found at Vathypetro.

In the central palace building at Archanes the number and variety of altars, sacred Horns of Consecration, and double-axe bases shows that religious ceremonies were performed both indoors (the upper floor of Room 10, and Rooms 4 and 17) and outdoors, especially on the «Platform» in the courtyard between Areas 1 and 11 where libations were made.

Certain ceremonies within the palace would have been attended only by a few people and involved both bloodless offerings (exemplified by the vases), and blood sacrifices indicated by the double-axe bases and the host of animal bones in Areas 10 and

37. Gold ring from Tholos Tomb A at Phourni.

38. Steatite seal-stone with a depiction of a griffin. From Tourkoyeitonia.

39. Sard seal-stone with a depiction of animals. From the Mycenaean Grave Enclosure.

17, and by the stone sacrificial altar with the tripodal offering tables from the upper floor of Room 10. The clay trays containing bones are clear evidence for just such a sacrifice as are the crypts of Area 17 where chthonic deities may have been worshiped. Other ritual ceremonies would likewise have had only a small attendance: for example, the symbolic «bathing» of the xoanon where only a simple sprinkling of the statue may have taken place with sacred jugs or rhytons. Those ceremonies associated with «ritual communion» of a variety of beverages drunken from a special goblet (as in the «Parisienne» fresco from Knossos) were performed by a select group, while the deity was invoked by blowing a horn made from a triton shell; a scene represented on a seal from the Idaean Cave.

On the other hand, ceremonies did exist in which more people took part, and these were mostly as-

sociated with populous ritual meals (see, for example, the finds from Area 19). The most famous of these ritual performances was «bull-leaping» where the taming of the beast involved not only men, but also women dressed in men's loincloths. The same ritual character was undoubtedly shared by the wrestling matches which, according to Evans, also occurred in the open air in front of a crowd of spectators. Water deities were worshiped during special ceremonies at the circular Reservoir. The aqueous qualities associated with the bull in Greek times (linking it to river gods, water and Poseidon) must have had their origins in Minoan times.

The appearance of the priest-king during processions for the offering of gifts by local governors or foreign embassies must have been especially impressive with his ornate loincloths and long women's vestments which enabled him to participate in the rituals of the female priesthood. Princes and officials wore tiaras and elaborate wigs with snake-like braids, as well as bracelets and neckbands; on their garments they wore sacred knots or nets. No doubt these trappings would have been worthy of the sumptuous venue.

Mention should also be made of ceremonies involving mime dances performed in the Theatre Area. Here dancers wore ritual animal masks, feathers attached to their shoulders, and animal skin costumes similar to those known from Egypt and Mesopotamia. When grouped together, these dancers may have represented a pantheon of various manifestations of the single deity. These rites were related to the fertility cycle encountered with variations (or at a different stage of development) in the worship of the «sacred tree» depicted on the Archanes gold ring. The gesture with upraised arms encountered in figurines has been interpreted as an act of exorcism, an attribute also said to explain the pose of figures holding garlands below the breast, the so-called *hypothymides* of the Greeks associated in later times with Artemis Diktyna or Europa Elotis, and possibly related to the remedial qualities of certain plants. These rites took place according to the seasons and - as we know from neighbouring civilizations such as Egypt - were accompanied by special ecstatic magic dances. Lucian refers to the survival of Minoan dances in the Greek period: the «round» dance (the *kyklos* of Hesychius), the *krinon* (lily) and *votrydon* (cluster of grapes), all names which suggest the formation taken by the dancers. The *telesias* was a sword-dance reminiscent of the *kybesteres*, or sword-jumping, known from Minoan depictions. Dances of lamentation referred to by Lucian were accompanied by hair-pulling and breast-beating and are associated with mourning ceremonies also known from Minoan depictions, notably in that masterpiece of Minoan art, the gold ring from Archanes depicting a mourning figure fallen over a baetyl. On the same ring a strapping figure touches or plants a tree, perhaps an olive, while the whole group is blessed by the Minoan goddess or her representative priestess. It is not impossible that the scene represents some mimetic ritual, es pecially when we remember that the mime dances of death and regeneration of the Greek period are directly associated with the fertility cycle.

Certain ritual ceremonies may have begun in the palace and continued elsewhere in shrines or at the cemetery since utensils of the same type have been found in all three areas. The seistrum from Funerary Building 9 in the Phourni cemetery bears certain proof of such rites, while Area 21 at Phourni and the vats for defiled wastes in the palace have a clear chthonic character through their physical contact with the chthonic deity.

Initiation rituals for boys, and possibly girls, constituted another important ceremony which was accompanied by shaving the initiant's head, a rite known from figurines found at Archanes and evident in contemporary Thera, Egypt and the East; during the Greek period it also appears at Sparta, Cretan Dreros and in the Attic rite of the Oskophoria. The initiation ceremony was followed by a change in clothing analogous to that made after Christian baptism. The next stage included contests such as boxing and the «grape- races», which also had a religious character. Bull-leaping may have been one of these contests since we know that a young girl is shown taking part in one of the depiction's of this sport. Initiation ceremonies would have taken place in small areas such as Area 4 and amongst a close circle; the ensuing contests took place in the courtyards. These rituals were followed by mass weddings, while symposia in large areas such as Area 19 would have followed sacrifices at altars appropriate for each occasion. Finally, flowers, branches and fruit would be deposited thereon, as depicted in the Archanes fresco.

Other ceremonies included apotropaic rituals with the binding of sacred trees in courtyards or sacred groves by priests wearing masks and dressed in bright long vestments or animal skins. The kings would have worn a heavily embroidered loin cloth girdled by netting with small weights, and would have been adorned with anklets, bracelets and a diadem.

The appearance of the queen-priestess would have occurred in the manner of an epiphany from a balcony in upper reaches of the palace, or from a height in the sacred grove or peak sanctuary.

The excavations at Archanes have brought with them a greater understanding of Minoan civilisation, highlighting as they do the zest for life, the colour, brilliance and splendour that imbued the entire settlement.

THE DESTRUCTION OF THE PALACE AND THE LATER PHASES

The palace at Archanes, built at around 1900 B.C. along with all the other Cretan palaces, did not escape their fate: catastrophic destruction.

Kamares ware found in the settlement shows that the Old Palace period was as brilliant as that of the new. An initial destruction by earthquake occurred at about the end of MM II (*ca.* 1700 B.C.), an event confirmed by the temple at Anemospilia which was destroyed at this time and never rebuilt. Hardly had the palaces been rebuilt when another earthquake struck at around 1600 B.C. At this time polychrome glazed pottery was still predominant, although the LM I Floral Style had already begun to be introduced. The causes of this catastrophe should be attributed to an earthquake occurring in the wake of the volcanic eruption on the island of Thera. In a short time, however, the entire island of Crete had recovered, and country villas now served as seats of local governors: in Archanes one such building was built at Vathypetro. The final catastrophe occurred in around 1450 B.C.

The excavations at Archanes are interesting for determining the date of this catastrophe since they have provided new and strong evidence that helps set Minoan chronology on firmer foundations. More specifically: it has long been accepted that Evans was correct to place the catastrophe prior to the introduction of the LH II Helladic style into Crete, which was introduced by the Mycenaean dynasty after the Achaean conquest but confined only to Knossos, whence its epithet «Palace Style». Recent excavations, however, have shown that this style existed in other areas although little consideration has been paid to the fact. In other words, LM II pottery has been found both in east and west Crete in conjunction with Marine Style pottery (or LM IB in general). Moreover, the palace at Archanes provided evidence of a mixture of styles on a single vase. Thus it is more than certain that the so-called «Palace Style» originated in Crete prior to the final catastrophe.

After the destruction of the palace, Archanes witnessed a new and splendid age under the Mycenaean dynasty. In the palace itself, as well as in the wider settlement with its hamlets and cemeteries and especially in the royal cemetery at Phourni, the fine funerary offerings bear clear testimony to a flourishing and prosperous society, although a more martial character is hinted at by increase in weaponry.

At around 1200 B.C., yet another terrible catastrophe, perhaps once more involving a natural phenomenon, brought with it a decline in population and the abandonment of most of the prehistoric sites.

THE CEMETERY AT PHOURNI

INTRODUCTION

The Minoan cemetery at Phourni is one of the most important archaeological sites in Crete. Excavations undertaken for over a quarter-of-a-century, and still underway, have uncovered 26 structures, mostly funerary buildings and including five tholos, or vaulted, tombs, although structures for cult and lay use were also found.

The cemetery's use for over a thousand years from the EM II period around 2400 B.C. to LM IIIC at about 1200 B.C. would have been enough to make it unique. But other singular qualities can also be indicated: the number and variety of funerary buildings concentrated in a single area and consisting of all known architectural types in which hundreds of burials were made, sometimes of distinguished royal personages, as well as the wealth and variety of the funerary offerings, most of which are now in the Herakleion Museum. Furthermore, the impressive amount of information on burial customs and tomb cult practices gathered during the excavations have provided a landmark for research, while on a more practical level our knowledge of the organisation and function of the cemetery itself is enriched with its ancillary buildings, paved roads, and even systems for the drainage of rain water. Equally intriguing is the association of data provided by this realm of the dead with that provided by the world of the living in the palatial centre, the Minoan settlement and the shrines. Finally, the cemetery's many imported objects provide information on contacts between Archanes and the Cyclades, Egypt and the East.

Little justification is thus needed to understand why this cemetery has been called «the most significant...in Crete», and «without exception one of the most important cemeteries of the Cretan-Mycenaean Aegean.» Even a brief foray there provides the visitor with a wealth of knowledge while at the same time allowing him to spend some time in an unspoilt part of Crete little changed since Minoan times. With painstaking care, an area of about five acres of vineyards, cypresses, and pine, olive and laurel trees has been transformed into one of the most beautiful archaeological sites in Crete, a veritable archaeological garden.

Until 1964, Phourni was unknown. Excavations conducted in that year by J. Sakellarakis on the eastern foot of the hill uncovered a tholos tomb; the first cenotaph of Minoan Crete. In 1965, Tholos Tombs A and B were located. Indeed, the side-chamber of the former providing archaeologists with the first undisturbed royal tomb in Crete. Excavations at the cemetery have continued from that time until today, and investigations are by no means over given that the cemetery's boundaries have not yet been discovered. One thing is certain: they did not extend westwards to the jagged and rocky summit of the hill.

Phourni is a small hill north-west of the modern town between Epano and Kato Archanes. The etymology of the name *Phourni* is clear: it comes from the word *phournos* (oven) and perhaps should be associated with the protrusion of the upper part of Tholos Tomb A which used to be visible to locals prior to the excavations.

Phourni delineates the small fertile plain of Archanes from the north-west since it lies to the north-east of Iouktas. However, it is not a forehill since a deep ravine divides it from the mountain. The western part of the hill is precipitous while the summit, wide at some points, is barren. Its eastern extent, however, is lush with grape-vines and olive trees.

The Minoan cemetery was founded on the summit and eastern side of the southern part of the hill nearest to Epano Archanes where the Minoan palace and settlement were located. The proximity of town and cemetery is reflected by that of their modern counterparts which preserve the same distance between them, but to the south.

There is no doubt that the approach to the Minoan cemetery throughout its history was made from the south, where the distance dividing it from the settlement was shortest. It is typical that the entrances of all the cemetery buildings should open to this direction. A wide pathway is still preserved today which leads from Kato Archanes to Phourni, and is paved where the way becomes

steep and uphill. It greatly resembles a paved uphill road uncovered in the Minoan cemetery itself.
It is thus possible that this wide path was constructed in Minoan times to function for centuries
as the cemetery road used, amongst other things,
for carrying the dead and sarcophagi.

The present approach to Phourni is made precisely from this ancient path which one encounters
intersecting the modern sign- posted road beginning from the entry to Epano Archanes. For those
who prefer going by car, the approach can also
be made from the agricultural road commencing
from the exit to Kato Archanes.

It is better to start a visit to the cemetery at
Phourni from the north going south, namely beginning with the Mycenaean Grave Enclosure and
terminating at Tholos Tomb D. This itinerary does
not follow any chronological order, a difficult task
seeing as the Minoans erected their funerary buildings wherever room was available. Furthermore,
some of these, as we shall see, were used for
hundreds of years.

All the funerary buildings have undergone structural support. The visitor should, however, take
care when visiting those many funerary buildings
preserved at a great height. These buildings were
numbered with arabic numerals in accordance with
the order in which they were excavated, with the
exception of the Mycenaean Grave Enclosure
which, apart from its numbering, was so-named
due to its distinctive architectural type. Likewise
the five tholos tombs (in addition to the general
number they have as structures) were styled
Tholos Tombs A to E in order of discovery, since
they belong to a separate architectural type. Consequently, the buildings which include burials are
named «Funerary Buildings» while those which had
civil, cult or unspecified use are termed simply
«Buildings».

DESCRIPTION OF THE BUILDINGS

The Mycenaean Grave Enclosure

In the northern-most section of the cemetery
excavated so far lies the Mycenaean Grave

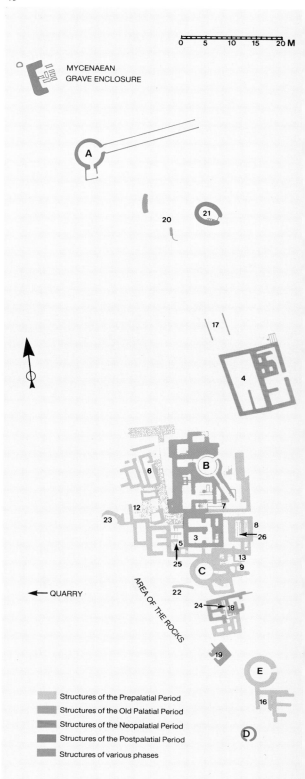

40

40. Plan of the Phourni cemetery.

41. *View of the Mycenaean Grave Enclosure, from the north.*

Enclosure (Funerary Building 11), a burial complex as yet without parallel in Crete containing seven LM III A graves from the 14th century B.C.

Of the rectangular enclosure, only the bottom course of the west and two small parts of the north and south wall are preserved towards the east, thus forming a Pi shape. Within the enclosure, seven rectangular graves were cut symmetrically into the soft rock at regular distances along three different rows. On the furthermost row to the west there is only one shaft, on the second, two, and on the third to the east, four. All share an east-west orientation with the exception of a shaft in the second row which lies north to south. The slope of the ground to the east is such that sufficient remains of this part of the enclosure have not been preserved and thus our knowledge of the nature of this section remains incomplete. At a small distance to the east there are traces of a wall lying almost parallel to the west enclosure wall although it is not certain whether this wall should be identified as part of the same complex.

However, entrance to the enclosure would have been made from the east.

The excavations showed that a sarcophagus (or *larnax* as they are more commonly known in Minoan archaeology) was placed inside each of the shafts at a small distance from the walls. All seven larnakes bore painted decoration but were found broken and empty, and of those still *in situ*, one of the long sides and the base was missing. In one case, a larnax had been emptied and then buried in the shaft. The larnakes were nearly all empty: only one provided small fragments of bone and a little jewelery consisting of beads of gold, sard, agate, glass paste, and faience. On the other hand, many finds were made of funerary offerings made during the burials and placed within the shafts but outside the larnakes. Thus it seems possible that the graves had not in fact been robbed but that after burial, the dead were exhumed and their bones deposited in the shafts on the broken bases of the larnakes.

All the burials were richly endowed with offerings, typical examples being a group of twelve bronze vessels. Four of these were preserved intact in Shaft 4, the so-called «Shaft of the Bronze Objects» (a jar, a basin, a ladle, and a two- hand-

42. Reconstruction of the burial in Shaft 4 of the Mycenaean Grave Enclosure.

led semi-globular vessel). Another five were found in a fragmentary state in Shaft 5, the «Shaft of the Bronze and Ivory Objects.» As we shall see, the only parallel for these finds are the ten bronze vessels uncovered in the undisturbed royal tomb in the side-chamber of Tholos Tomb A. Two stone vases were found in Shaft 2 (one large cylindrical vessel with a wide spout, and a small globular vase of Egyptian diorite): this was the «Shaft of the Stone Vases». Other shafts gave up extremely important ivory objects belonging to inlays or cosmetic instruments: a large ivory pyxis and lid, the latter with a relief lion decoration, and a bronze mirror with an ivory handle depicting in relief a cow suckling her calf, and yet again corresponding to a similar example found in the side-chamber of Tholos Tomb A. An ivory comb was also found decorated on either side with successive relief lizards. Finally, of the three exceptional lentoid seal-stones discovered, one made of amethyst was «talismanic» and decorated with ivy leaves with a central star, the second of sard with a wonderful naturalistic rendition of three goats, and the third, also of sard but fragmentary, with a goat being chased by another animal.

The importance of the burials as evinced by the wealth, variety and quality of the funerary offerings is highlighted by the funerary stelai erected above them, something almost unrecorded in Crete. Roughly worked slabs were found in Shafts 2, 3, and 5 and evidently had fallen thither from the top. The case of Shaft 2 is characteristic: the stele had fallen along its length with its base facing west. It was precisely in the western part of this cutting that the only skull fragments and a few teeth were found. Thus the stele had been erected over the head of the body, with its better- finished side facing east towards the entrance.

The discovery of these three funerary *stelai* in the Mycenaean Grave Enclosure is of great importance not only for their association with the stelai of Mycenaean Greece (whether in relief, painted or plain) but also for the study of the origins of later Greek funerary stelai, given that the Archanes examples are of a particularly early date. The existence of grave markers would also have necessitated the construction of the enclosure. Here, then, we have evidence for the simultaneous building

45

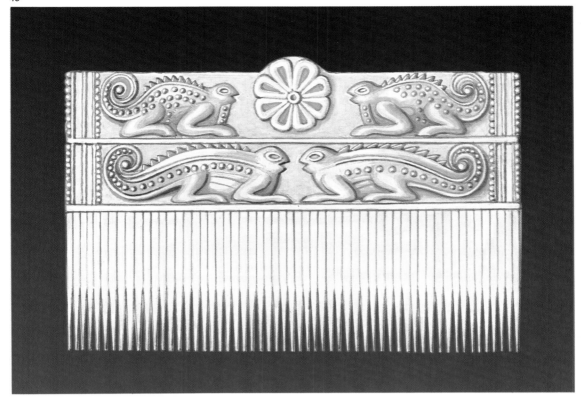

43. *The bronze vessels of Shaft 4, as they were found between the walls of the larnax and the sides of the shaft.*

44. *The bronze vessels of Shaft 4 of the Mycenaean Grave Enclosure.*

45. *Ivory comb from the Mycenaean Grave Enclosure (accurate graphic reconstruction).*

of the enclosure, sinking of the shaft graves and interment of the larnakes.

The Mycenaean Grave Enclosure is unique in Crete, both as a single entity and by virtue of its piecemeal components. Although rare, Mycenaean shaft burials are not unknown on the island, being mostly encountered in Knossian cemeteries contemporary to the Archanes enclosure. Naturally, they area considered to be the result of Mycenaean influence. But the Knossian shafts were dug at various points in the cemetery along with other grave types, and thus any parallel with the Phourni enclosure must be sought outside Crete: in the royal Grave Circles A and B at Mycenae itself where funerary stelai were also erected over certain shafts.

The burials of the Mycenaean enclosure are, of course, much older than those at Archanes. However, it is interesting that the circles enclosing the royal tombs at Mycenae were erected at a later date, perhaps at a period slightly after the construction of the Phourni enclosure wall. The difference in shape between the Mycenae and Phourni walls is due to the random placement of the graves in the former, which consequently could only have been surrounded by a circular structure. The case is quite different at Phourni with the regular alignment of its shaft graves. The basic idea is, however, common to both: to pay respect to certain graves by constructing an enclosure wall for their protection as well as marking them with stelai. The question of tomb cult practices in Grave Circle A at Mycenae is still much debated, as is the correct interpretation of the circular *bothros*, or reservoir-like structure, in the same complex. The discovery of a similar structure in the Phourni enclosure is consequently of some import.

At a small distance outside the enclosure to the north-west, a circular pit some 2.70m. was dug into the rock and lined with walls of large stones and a slab floor. The mouth of this pit is formed by stone slabs lying flat in a circular arrangement on the ground. Within this pit were various pottery fragments that appear to be libation vessels. Typical of these is a large one-handled cup with a wide spout and some form of plastic decoration on the inner base. The absence of other finds, and of bones in particular, is noteworthy since this probably indicates that what we have here is a bothros intended only for the deposition of liquid offerings. During excavations of the pit, it was found that the soil therein, especially in the deeper levels, was of a different texture to that found elsewhere in the cemetery and, indeed, exuded an unbearable stench, suggesting its having been drenched with various kinds of liquid over time. Finally, another indication of its use was provided by the numerous sherds from small vessels, notably cups, found on the surface around the pit, quite unlike the case with the enclosure where such finds were scanty.

Here for the first time the existence of a bothros is encountered in a Cretan cemetery. It may have been used in tomb cult rituals such as the libations mentioned by Homer (*Odyssey*, XI 24-28):

«*...while I drew my sharp sword from beside my thigh, and dug a pit of a cubit's length this way and that, and around it poured a libation to all the dead, first with milk and honey, thereafter with sweet wine, and in the third place with water...*»

(Loeb translation)

This should not seem strange since, as we shall see, not a few areas in the cemetery bear traces of practices associated with the veneration of the dead. The Mycenaean Grave Enclosure at Archanes is thus especially significant since it confirms that the dead interred therein were not simply respected personages, but figures who were deemed worthy of worship; namely members of the island's Achaean aristocracy.

Tholos Tomb A

Tholos Tomb A with the undisturbed royal burial in its side- chamber was the first funerary building to be found and excavated at Phourni in 1965. This discovery, which led to that of the unique cemetery complex itself, was nothing short of remarkable. Prior to the excavations, a «hut» had always been visible on the site and had been utilised by the local inhabitants for various farming uses. During the last War it even served as a hiding place. On the outside it did indeed resemble a stone-built «hut» of some kind with a door facing east, and as such was visible from the Herakleion-Archanes arterial road. To the trained eye, however, matters were somewhat different. For the «hut» was nothing less than the Archanes Tholos Tomb A, constructed in the 14th century B.C. and shelter for a royal burial in its side- chamber.

With the passage of time both the tomb's tholos and *dromos* (or approach) had been filled with earth up to the lintel of the entrance. The tomb's ceiling still bears clear traces of the level reached by the fill, and of the upper section which once passed for a «hut», now intensely green and worn due to long exposure to the elements. The original lintel of the dromos was used as a threshold for the «hut». It is certain that the «hut's» door was initially a hole opened in the tholos by Roman or even Minoan grave-robbers (on which more below) and repaired by the villagers with rubble at a later date.

The ground plan of Tholos Tomb A at Archanes is unique in Crete, consisting of a dromos orientated east to west, a tholos and a side-chamber to the south on the left. In other words, it shares the same ground plan with two of the most important tholos tombs of Mycenaean Greece, the so-called «Treasuries» of Atreus at Mycenae and Minyas at Orchomenos.

Tholos Tomb A is also the best preserved of the tholos tombs in Crete, perhaps due to a huge slab used as a finial block at the heart of the vault. The roof, whose outer surface has been cleaned, is of great interest, even for tholos tombs of Mycenaean Greece. For example, the vertical slabs around the periphery of the tholos may have functioned to collect the earth of the tumulus which covered the monument.

The tomb's dromos is dug into the soft kouskoura rock and is one of the longest tholos tomb dromoi in Crete. The entrance to the tholos was tall and narrow, without a threshold, and filled in to the massive lintel with large stones that were removed only with the greatest difficulty. As with all Mycenaean tholos tombs, the lintel was located at a point corresponding to ground level on the upper parts of the dromos walls. It is possible that, as with the large finial block employed in the vault, the key-stone was hewn on the spot from the adjacent rocks (whose strata are still visible) and thus needed only to be dragged into position, not hoisted.

The dromos did not give up notable finds apart

46

46. *View of Tholos Tomb A, from the east.*

47. *The excavation of Tholos Tomb A (oil-painting by M. Fioraki).*

47

from the section just in front of the entrance. Here a number of well- worked upright blocks were found situated parallel to each other in a regular arrangement at equal distances. With them were found course pottery fragments from the Roman period, mostly of domestic ware, some certainly coming from cooking utensils. A few finer vases were also found. These sherds together with some lamp fragments point to temporary occupation in Roman times.

Some explanation is needed as to why people should have been present in a Minoan cemetery during the Roman period and, moreover, at such a depth before the entrance of a tholos tomb. This is not an isolated instance since glass fragments from Roman vessels and bracelets were also found on the cemetery's surface. Perhaps these sporadic Roman finds belonged not to visitors to the long-disused cemetery, but to grave-robbers who may have been attracted by a chance

48

49

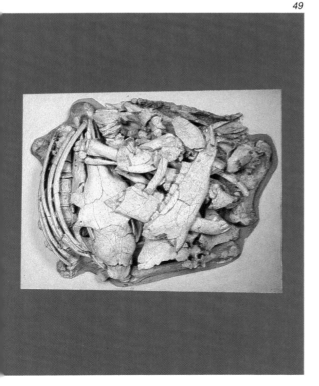

discovery in the area. Thus the remains found in front of the entrance to the Tholos Tomb A may be relics of an unsuccessful attempt at pillage.

The tholos, 4.31m. in diameter, was roughly built with circular horizontal layers of large semi-finished stone blocks, some measuring 1m. long. At the base, the walls are vertical but from a certain point they begin to incline towards the centre in order to form the tholos which is 5.04m. high, the highest in Crete. It is certain that no relieving triangle gap existed above the lintel on the original. However, two large blocks to the south, conveniently placed amongst the cantilevered horizontal courses, relieve the lintel of the low doorway into the side- chamber, a feature which accords with attested Mycenaean techniques. As with the central entrance doorway, that of the side-chamber was blocked up to its lintel with unworked stones, although of a somewhat looser construction. The entrance to the side-chamber is lower than the main doorway and thus had to be relieved from the correspondingly greater weight above.

The almost unified fill of the tholos up to the lintel consisted of stones thrown into the opening above by generations of farmers. The spaces left between these stones provided ideal nests for snakes (not generally encountered elsewhere at Phourni) whose number was so great during the first excavations, slipping this way and that amongst the stones, that the workmen initially refused to dig there, adding yet another obstacle to what had already proved a difficult task.

Finds were very few. One charming specimen is a Venetian coin, unique amongst the finds at Phourni and perhaps left by some Renaissance traveller searching for the tomb of Zeus. The stone fill went down to floor level, and stones were even found in a rectangular pit (dimensions 1.44 x 0.56m. and 0.32m. deep) dug askew into the

48. *Detail of the bull sacrifice scene on the Aghia Triada larnax.*

49. *The skeleton of the slaughtered horse, as found in Tholos Tomb A.*

50. *Reconstruction of part of Tholos Tomb A showing the location of members of the sacrificed animals, a horse and a bull, on the Tholos floor and in the fill of the side-chamber doorway respectively.*

51. The larnax of the side-chamber of Tholos Tomb A.

southern section of the tholos floor, just in front of the side-chamber entrance. The pit is no longer visible since it hindered the approach to the chamber. For this reason, and to protect the monument in general, it was filled with earth as was – to a certain height – the tholos floor. Found inside this pit were large pieces of a terracotta Late Minoan larnax decorated with the ritual motif of the Horns of Consecration. This would indicate that burials had been made within the tholos proper but had been thoroughly robbed.

All the other burial remains in the tholos had been completely and carefully removed indicating that the robbers not only had the time and comfort to lift their spoils up to the opening above the lintel, but also that they could clearly see all the burial objects. Since this would mean that the latter could not have been covered with fill, it is possible that the tomb was robbed during Minoan times while the burials were uncovered and all the

perishable materials therein had only begun the process of decay.

The only part of the tholos tomb which remained undisturbed was that between the pit and the wall to the right of the side- chamber entrance. It was here that one of the most remarkable, and in many ways unique, finds of animal remains in Crete was made: the dismembered skeleton of a horse. It is beyond doubt that the animal was slaughtered and systematically dismembered with the greatest care. The head was separated from the neck, the legs from the body, and the sides from the spinal cord. The bottom jaw was split from the skull and divided into two. Even remains of the haunch were cut away. The bones of the animal's back bore clear traces of blows with a sharp instrument, probably a knife. More interesting was the fact that after the disemboweling, all the pieces were gathered together and carefully placed in the tomb; even the legs were bent at the knee.

The horse was about six years old and of the species *equus caballus*. The place, period and manner of the horse's slaughter are significant,

52

especially when it is taken into account that the rib bones found *in situ* indicate that the members were deposited while flesh was still attached. In short, we undoubtedly have here a horse-sacrifice in honour of the person buried in the side chamber.

When the upper stones were removed from the blockage to the side-chamber entrance, even more significant animal remains were uncovered in the form of the skull of a bull. This was found hidden between the stones at an angle to the main tholos chamber with the nozzle upwards and the jaw facing the side-chamber. Zoologists have identified the skull as belonging to the species *bos primigenius*.

Detailed study indicated that the skull was the relic of a bull-sacrifice and had, like the horse, been slaughtered in honour of the person buried in the side-chamber. Once again, the place, period and manner of this sacrifice is of especial importance for the study of religion in Minoan Crete not only because bull-sacrifices were the most common and important in Minoan Crete, but also

52. Reconstruction of the location of the larnax and the offerings thereabouts, in the side-chamber of Tholos Tomb A.

since problems associated with the till-then poorly interpreted depiction on the famous Aghia Triada larnax were clarified.

One side of the Aghia Triada larnax depicts a bull-sacrifice. Scholars had long been perplexed by the fact that rituals rendered to the deity should be depicted on a funerary monument such as this. The Archanes bull-sacrifice, however, showed that divine worship (and, moreover, the sacrifice of a sacred beast such as a bull) could be rendered up to living beings but only if they could in life have enjoyed divine honours: namely, the priest-kings and members of the royal family. Without a doubt, one such person was the woman interred in the side-chamber of Tholos Tomb A at Archanes, as we shall see below.

The discovery of the bull-sacrifice during the excavations of 1965 made the existence of a side-chamber in Tholos Tomb A a possibility. Behind the outer blockage fill of the inner doorway, however, a second wall was found through whose stones the naked rock was visible. The removal of this wall was impossible since the entire monument was so unsound as to be in danger of collapse. No other choice remained but to excavate from the top downwards from outside. The side-chamber as it appears today in its restored state is most deceptive in giving any idea of the uncertainty involved in this operation. For it was still not clear whether, in fact, a side-chamber carved into the rock actually existed, while the «opening» uncovered inside the tholos may have been a false door, not unknown from other Cretan tholos tombs. Patience and hard work had their reward, however, when at a depth of 4.90m. below surface level the initial fragments of Crete's first undisturbed royal tomb came to light.

The ensuing excavations showed that the rock-cut trapezoidal side-chamber measuring only 3.67 square metres contained a single burial in a clay larnax. A great number of important finds were found within, beneath and around the larnax. After the larnax was placed along the south wall of the chamber, it became necessary to utilise the now restricted space in a careful and orderly manner.

The larnax is one of the largest ever found in Crete till now. Traces of yellowish plaster at many places on the lid and handles indicate that it had been sealed. The sealing must have occurred after the lid had been secured by tightening of the ropes threaded through the handles at the corners. This action may have been taken for purely practical reasons in order to protect the living from the odours of putrefaction. It is not impossible on the other hand that it was related to older burial customs aimed at preventing the escape of the deceased's spirit.

Fortunately, a few remains of the skeleton helped preserve the burial position, with the head facing west and the pose in the foetus position. Thus the exact location on the body of the mostly gold small objects, mostly belonging to necklaces, could be established. Two groups of gold bead were also discovered, one in the shape of rosettes and the other in the form of small palmette-shaped papyri. These had without doubt been sewn onto a garment since the first group was found at the waist along the length of the body, and the second along the length of the legs. The person buried here would have worn a long ankle-length, gold-trimmed ritual gown similar to that known from figures depicted on wall- paintings where the vertical and horizontal fringes of similar garments are adorned with like motifs.

Apart from the two groups of small finds mentioned above, nearly all the others were found around the breast. These included, together with the necklaces: three gold signet-rings, a gold clasp, a gold ring and two small gold caskets. Also found in the larnax were two iron beads, a much oxidized bronze lentoid seal-stone with indiscernible decoration, another seal-stone made of sard depicting two goats, a faience pin, fragments of a faience vase and two steatite whorls.

All the remaining objects were placed outside the larnax. So as to leave an empty space in front of the larnax seven of the ten bronze vases in the chamber were neatly piled in the south-east corner, one on top of the other. This is a unique find for Crete, if one excepts the so-called «Tomb of the Tripod Hearth» at Knossos. The first vessel to be deposited, upside-down, seems to have been the bronze tripod cauldron with its legs jutting upwards. Placed askew in front of this were three bronze vessels: a jug with a relief band of shells at the shoulder, a large two-handled bowl, and another jug with a band at the shoulder adorned with argonaut motifs. Between the upturned legs of the tripod there was a large two-handled plain tripod vase and another small two-handled bowl. Finally, beside and slightly to the front of this pile was a large bronze hydria. The care taken in positioning the bronze vessels helped preserve them in very good condition.

Of the three small bronze vases found under the larnax, the first was a lamp, the second a cup and the third a small plain vase with a vertical handle. Also found under the larnax was a decorated bronze implement with an ivory handle and a host of ivory fragments, possibly part of the dressing from seven now disintegrated wooden vessels. A mirror with an ivory handle bearing a relief depiction of a cow suckling her calf was found between the south wall and the larnax, and was evidently thrown there from above.

Finds from the royal burial in the side-chamber of Tholos Tomb A: 53. A gold ring with a cult scene, 54: Two small ornate gold caskets which served as amulets or charms, 55: A sard seal-stone with a depiction of wild-goats.

53

54

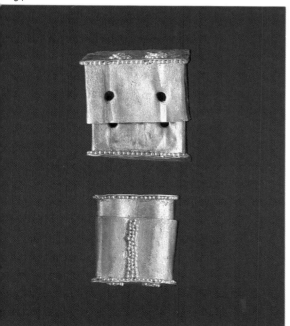

55

*Finds from the royal burial in the side-chamber of Tholos
Tomb A: 56. A sard necklace, 57: Necklaces made of
glass-paste, 58: Gold necklaces and attached ornaments.*

56

Along the west wall and in front of the larnax were eight carefully positioned small clay vases. At the south-west corner was another smaller pile, this time of glass-paste beads belonging to a necklace and including gold beads and two gold finger-rings. The rings had obviously been suspended from the necklace since they were intertwined when found, as if still held by the thread.

Finally, along the front of the larnax to the west lay the remnants of one of the most important and, for Crete, unique of the undisturbed tomb's offerings: a footstool. The remains consisted of 87 ivory fragments which would have adorned the front panel of this wooden piece of furniture. Naturally, the wood has disintegrated but the position of the ivory fragments where they fell had not been disturbed, thus making it possible to reconstruct the footstool's original composition with precision. The protruding handles thereon were decorated with relief heads of helmeted Mycenaean warriors.

The object is 35cm. long, just enough to serve as a footstool. It corresponds precisely to the «ta-ra-nu» on the Linear B inscriptions from Pylos, namely the Homeric *threnyes*: the footstools made of ebony with ivory inlays and decorated with human figures. The general shape of the rectangular Archanes footstool with its protruding human heads is the same as that delineated by the ideogram on the Linear B tablets and even corresponds to a depiction of the same object on a large gold ring from Tiryns.

It is characteristic that the footstool should be placed by itself just in front of the larnax and together with a stone vase to the left, while all the other objects noted were piled into corners. This may have been done to free the front space for some ritual ceremony which followed the interment of the larnax, ceremonies in which the

59. Various ivory objects in the arrangement they were found in the side-chamber of Tholos Tomb A. Together they constitute the inlay decoration from the front of a footstool.

60. One of the Mycenaean warrior heads made from boar's tusk which decorated the handles of the footstool.

59

footstool may have been used. It is more likely, however, that the single stone vase was used together with its many clay substitutes at the end of these rituals.

The exceptional importance of the Tholos Tomb A side-chamber burial derives not only from the significant information gathered during the course of excavation, or even from the remarkable funerary offerings, but from the light thrown on many specific subjects associated with Minoan Crete during the Mycenaean period, and, indeed, with the Cretan-Mycenaean world in general.

The poor state of the skeletal remains are hardly conducive to providing anthropological information on the sex and age of the side-chamber's occupant. The finds, on the other hand, are quite a different matter. The absence of weapons, the many domestic utensils and of course the wealth of the jewelery clearly point to this being the burial of a woman.

The finds suggest the social rank of this woman since it is generally accepted that the amount of

funerary offerings reflects the position enjoyed by the deceased during his or her life. This woman's burial, adorned as she was with a long gold-trimmed garment, is without parallel in Crete. The amount of gold and other jewelery found is almost as much as that found in all the contemporary chamber tombs at Knossos, and, of course, is richer than other similar burials in the Knossian cemetery. Moreover, the iron beads (the only specimens known from this period due to the rarity of the material) could only have served to adorn the most distinguished of people. In all the Cretan-Mycenaean world, no other burial has been found to date with a total of five gold signet-rings together with two more seals of bronze and sard - seven in all and each perhaps covering a variety of functions. Important social rank is further stressed by the fact that burial took place in a side-chamber, an exceptional honour generally accepted as being the privilege of royalty. There is no doubt that the woman entombed in the side chamber of Tholos Tomb A at Archanes was of royal blood.

Furthermore, the finds also point to the fact that this royal lady also held some priestly office. This is clear firstly from the depictions on the rings, one of which bears an important cult scene while the other four show the religious motif of the figure- of-eight shield in a variety of combinations; in one instance even with a sacred knot. It is no coincidence, perhaps, that the figure-of-eight shields should also appear on the sard seal-stone and the marvelously preserved footstool. But the deceased's identity as a queen-priestess is most powerfully attested by the sacrifices made in her honour, in particular that of the bull. Moreover, this double religious and civil nature is also attested in the shaft burial within the very same Tholos Tomb A where, as we saw, fragments of a larnax were found decorated with Horns of Consecration. As we shall see below, the nature of the burials in the royal grave building complex of Tholos Tomb B shared this double nature with those of Tholos Tomb A. Precisely for this reason it is not impossible that Building 21 – with its possible ritual use – near to the entrance to the dromos of Tholos Tomb A may have been associated with the latter in a specific manner, just as the bothros was with the Mycenaean Grave Enclosure.

The burial in the side-chamber of Tholos Tomb A must have taken place at the end of LM III A1, in the first half of the 14th century B.C. This date is interesting in as far as the indirect information it thus provides for the state of affairs in Crete, and in Archanes in particular, during these years.

After the final destruction of the palace at Knossos and the complete domination of the Mycenaeans, life on Crete not only failed to cease, but underwent a new period of ascent. Royal families continued to hold power in the old and well-known Minoan centres. At Archanes in particular with its venerable yet dynamic Minoan tradition, the Mycenaean dynasts were most powerful as we can tell from the amount of finds, the significant remains at Tourkoyeitonia, the important burials at Phourni (such as the Mycenaean Grave Enclosure), Tholos Tomb D and, of course, from the undisturbed royal burial in the side-chamber of Tholos Tomb A.

Building 21

Building 21 at Phourni is located slightly southeast of Tholos Tomb A and consists of a drop-shaped tholos structure with a descending stairway. Architecturally, it remains without parallel in the Minoan repertoire as we know it.

This was a subterranean structure with only the upper tip of its vaulted roof (now caved in) exposed to the open. The approach thereto was made from the south-east, at the narrowest point of the «drop» where the threshold joined the terminals of the walls. A stairway grounded on the rock commences from this point and leads into the building. The stairs follow the ellipse of the «drop» covering three-quarters of its total length. The last step ends at the building's western section at a large hollow in the rock 0.40m. deep and with a diameter of 1.45m. below and 1.90m. above. A channel 0.50m. wide carved into the rock follows the stairway and was perhaps used to support some wooden structure or to stand vases.

Unfortunately, the finds here throw no light on how this peculiar building should be interpreted. Found in the lowest level were large fragments of cooking pots and pithoi, sherds from medium sized vessels, jars, jugs, globular and conical cups, and ladles, all of which date the building's last phase of use to the end of the Mycenaean period, more specifically to LM IIIB around the 13th century B.C.

The strikingly original architectural construction of Building 21, unknown not only in Crete but in the entire Aegean area, makes this a very important structure. No other example exists of a subterranean «drop»-shaped tholos with a descending staircase. The theory that this should be regarded as a funerary building is not entertained for the simple reason that there is insufficient room for burials and associated functions, and furthermore no bones were found during excavation, nor were other remains uncovered which could even suggest burial use. Thus, this constitutes (after Building 4) the second building that may have been reserved for the use of the living in the service of the cemetery's needs.

Similar structures are known from Minoan palaces and houses; namely the characteristic feature of a closed underground crypt-like space approached by a descending stairway. These are the so- called Lustral Basins which are now more and more accepted as having had some ritual purpose. The chthonic nature of ritual is most natural in a cemetery context, and especially at Phourni, where, as we saw above, a similar bothros was uncovered for the libations made to the dead of the Mycenaean Grave Enclosure. Unlike the Lustral Basins, of course, Building 21 is not rectangular, but the structure may have been adapted to the common architectural tholos type found at Phourni. It should be noted that both in date of construction and in location it is close to Tholos Tomb A, undoubtedly of greater importance than the Mycenaean Grave Enclosure where the bothros for libations to the dead is a much more unassuming structure.

Building 20

A trial trench west of Building 21 and south of Tholos Tomb A brought to light yet another building unique in Crete: Building 20. An extent of 35m² is covered here by a floor some 0.50m. thick made of small stones. This pile of stones is surrounded by a sturdy circular wall, part of which was located to the north-west. Found amongst the stones were a few animal and human bones. More numerous by far were the MM IIIB - LM IA sherds from cups, tripod cooking pots, juglets, and shallow bowls. Amongst the many small finds which came to light were a band of silver and two stone vases, one of them a *kernos*. In the middle of the mass of stones an ellipsoidal structure 4.40m. long was encountered, together with possible traces of another. Prior to its full excavation, the use of this building cannot be hypothesised. However, the possibility should not be ruled out that a burial tumulus may have existed here such as those known till now only on mainland Greece.

Building 4

Almost in the centre of the cemetery's eastern side between Tholos Tombs A and B, and slightly closer and to the north-east of the latter, one encounters Building 4. Once again, we are confronted here with a building unique not only for Minoan but also more generally for Aegean cemeteries. Excavated finds showed that this building was used by the living for the care of the dead, probably during the LM IA period (*ca.* 1550-1500 B.C.)

Building 4 is a complex rectangular structure built on different levels and comprising of two separate wings, east and west. The west, and largest, rectangular wing is at a higher level and basically constitutes an integrated space with internal walls and a paved floor. The east wing is at a lower level (and thus better preserved) and is made up of two large rooms to the south and six small ones to the north. The two wings of Building 4, so different architecturally, evidently had different functions as their respective finds indicated. Thus it has been deemed wise to discuss them separately.

The east wing

The east wing was possibly built prior to the west wing, which it abutted.

Due to the terrain, the two southern-most rooms (Rooms 1 and 2) were level with the ground. However, the six small rooms to the north whose foundations were laid at a higher level, were in turn used as supports for the upper floor and even in the construction of a stairway thereto. From this point westwards the rock is noticeably higher. A large doorway almost in the centre of the outer east wall leads to Room 2 whence another entrance opens onto Room 1. Just following from the outer doorway of Room 2, another smaller doorway opens onto a corridor which seems to have led *via* a stairway to the upper story.

The existence of a storey which covered the entire eastern wing is confirmed by finds recovered from the fill, these naturally being more abundant in Rooms 1 and 2. The fact that similar objects were recovered from clearing operations outside the sturdy east wall indicates that part of the storey's contents also fell outside the building during the catastrophe. Thus the exact find location of objects in the fill suggests not only their original location on the upper floor but, more importantly, the clearly industrial utilisation of the floor's various areas.

No evidence was preserved for the arrangement of areas on the upper storey of the east wing. It is certain, however, that the interior walls were covered with painted plaster in various colours as well as band decoration. The size and impressive height of the wing, including the ground floor, together with its powerful external aspect gave the upper floor a dais-like appearance highlighted by the windows to the east, north and south. This feature is even more stressed by the structure's very location on the edge of the cemetery with its entrance facing the plain, the palace centre and the settlement.

In the central part of the floor to the south there once stood one or more looms from which 46 clay loom weights fell, mostly into Room 2, but also into Room 1. A few personal items also fell from this floor including a steatite seal-stone depicting lions, a sard amulet in the shape of a seated monkey, and a bead. Further south, the area must have been used for the storage of various goods since pieces of twelve fallen pithoi were also found. Fragments of two terracotta figurines indicate that some ritual function for the area cannot be ruled out. The various bronze objects which came to light would no doubt have originally been located north of the loom, in the centre of the wing (two knives, a cutter, a pin, a lead weight from a pair of scales, and, most importantly, a large ingot of bronze ready for processing). Pottery, of course, was also evident throughout including a few intact specimens of cups as well as steatite and diorite stone vases, blades, obsidian chips and cores, stone mortars and pestles of various sizes, and whetstones.

These finds make it abundantly clear that the entire floor of the eastern wing of Building 4 was given over to industrial activity which, as we shall see, is not unconnected with the function of the ground floor Rooms 1 and 2 in the same wing. Traces of a homestead are, moreover, quite clear on the ground floor.

The nature of the terrain necessitated that the six small rooms to the north be built on higher ground. They were in turn used as supports for the upper floor and for the creation of an approach thereto with a doorway and a possible small staircase immediately to the right and north of the large outer entrance. Only the two largest and most southerly rooms were on ground-level, and important finds were uncovered on the floor surface.

A clay utensil for squashing grapes was found *in situ* in Room 2. That the room had been specifically arranged for wine making is indicated by the fact that the rock was roughly carved into two levels: one at a lower level to the east which was used both as a floor and as a receptacle for the wine-must, and another at a higher level to the west where the clay wine-press was situated. Three large vases (two amphorae and a jug) were placed on the upper level towards the north wall. Of the three cooking pots found in the same spot, two were recovered from a higher deposit and

62

62. Clay loom weights from Building 4.

thus their original location on the ground floor is not certain.

An elliptical vat was constructed to the east to collect the must. The natural rock face left by the change in levels comprised the western end of this vat, while to the east a low curved wall of small stones and earth had been constructed. Two vessels found herein, an amphora and a cup, were undoubtedly used for collecting the liquid.

Beyond doubt, then, the ground-floor of Room 2 in the east wing of Building 4 was used as a wine-press of the same kind as known from other structures in Minoan Crete. Furthermore, it is noteworthy that two circular depressions of unequal depth sunk into the rock surface are of the same type as those used till only recently by the local villagers to collect even the last drops of the must from their own presses in Archanes, still so rich in grapes and wine. A hard material found within these depressions must be dried must.

Equally interesting finds came to light on the ground floor of neighbouring Room 1. In the room's south-east corner immediately opposite the doorway, a cylindrical pithos was found intact with eleven vases placed around it. Yet another vase was found in the doorway and another on the east wall. Finally, five olive pips were found on the floor next to a jar which may have originally contained them.

The two ground-floor rooms of the east wing of Building 4 are no doubt related. Perhaps after pressing, the wine must was stored in the large pithos in Room 1 while the vases found thereabouts were used to carry it. It is thus certain that, together with the upper floor, the ground floor of the east wing of Building 4 was also of an industrial nature. Prior to interpreting, however, the nature of this installation of the living in the resting place of the dead, the building's west wing must also be examined.

The west wing

As we have seen, the entire west wing is a large rectangular area built on higher ground straight onto the rock and without internal partitions, with the exception of a transverse wall to the south with a north-south orientation. To the north-north-west an extensive section of an area paved with large slabs covers the wing's foundation walls. This paved surface certainly continued east and south and may have covered the entire western wing. Perhaps, then, the transverse wall mentioned above belonged to the paving's foundations. Three important architectural members were found at various points along the side of the paved surface having fallen thence onto the natural rock: these were three stone column bases, a unique find for a Minoan cemetery and more generally for those in the Aegean area. It is thus possible that the west wing of Building 4 consisted of a paved surface open on all sides on the level of the eastern wing's upper storey and with an open colonnade along its length, hence the column bases.

This unprecedented architectural configuration in the central flat area of a cemetery was evidently meant as a venue suitable for the performance of funerary rites, an interpretation supported by the objects found therein. A thick fill between low loosely built rubble walls was found amongst the foundations of the paved surface in the area created to the east by the transverse wall. Here, a large amount of sherds and small finds were uncovered including part of a four-sided serpentine libation table and fragments of two bell-shaped figurines. More importantly, however, 250 small conical cups came to light placed upright or upside-down, a position which is known to indicate some ritual act.

The lack of bone remains indicates that Building 4 is certainly not a funerary building, and may not in fact be alone amongst the 26 buildings of the Phourni cemetery. Thus the first identification of a structure for the living in a Minoan cemetery, and indeed in any cemetery throughout the Aegean, cannot be passed over without comment. Of course, the industrial installations in Building 4 rule out its having been a simple house. The fact that it was erected amongst funerary buildings can only mean that it was intended for the manufacture of goods to be used in the burial of the dead. Until now, similar installations have only been known from Egypt where an array of industries for products used on the dead (such as shrouds) flourished in the well-organised cemeteries of the Nile delta.

Consequently, it is quite possible that people were installed in the cemetery to care for the dead. The wine produced would have been used not only for funerary meals but also for libations such as those we saw took place in the Mycenaean Grave Enclosure. It is worthy to note that in Egypt, the industries mentioned were under the supervision of the priesthood. This also seems to be the case at Archanes since both parts of Building 4, the ritual and the industrial, are in such a close proximity to warrant possible communication between both. Perhaps the foundation of Building 4 is not unrelated to the use of Tholos Tomb B during that period.

Building 17

North-west of Building 4, the foundations of two parallel walls running north to south were discovered, namely the remains of Building 17. The walls surrounded a loosely constructed paved surface under which rich pottery deposits were found, probably originating from a clearing of funerary

63. Reconstruction of the wine-press of Room 2 in Building 4, with the utensils and vessels in the location they were found.

64. The vat used for the squashing of grapes in Building 4.

buildings undertaken in MM IA and LM IA, and perhaps including that of Tholos Tomb B which, as we shall see, was used during the latter period.

The main deposit of LM IA pottery (*ca.* 1550-1500 B.C) had been made in a deep concavity carved from the natural rock. At least 120 vases came to light, intact or preserved to a great extent, including plain and one-handled conical cups, juglets, krateriskoi, skyphoi, jugs, cooking pots, jars, pitchers and amphora fragments, as well as parts of larger pithoid vessels and larnakes. The small finds included a few stone vase fragments and zoomorphic figurines. The surface deposits gave up a bronze coin and glass from the Roman period.

The paved surface found in Building 17 is not unrelated to the similar large surface of Building 4. Furthermore, there is the possibility that another paved surface existed on the rock to the north of the north wall of Building 4. It is certain that this area was open, and indeed had been used as an approach to the cemetery, since three large steps were found in the north-east corner of Building 4.

Tholos Tomb B

Tholos Tomb B is located south-west of Building 4 and constitutes the most important architectural structure in the cemetery at Phourni, not to mention the largest, tallest and most complex.

The Tholos Tomb B complex, built on the remains of the older Funerary Building 7, lies at the centre of that part of the cemetery excavated up till now, and on the widest and flattest part of the slope of Phourni. The tholos rises above ground to the east of Funerary Building 6, and north of Funerary Buildings 3 and 8. Characteristically, the areas around the building were left open, apart from the south side where Funerary Building 3 is located, while Building 4 was built close by and may have been associated with it.

A natural *terminus post quem* for the foundation of Tholos Tomb B is the date of the early MM IA Funerary Building 7 (after 2100 B.C.) on which it was built. A *terminus ante quem* is provided by the re-founding of the sturdy curtain wall between Funerary Building 6 and the western outer wall of Tholos Tomb B, from which hundreds of vases were discarded from the later MM IA period (*ca.* 2000 B.C.) It is thus certain that Tholos Tomb B was built at the end of the Early Bronze Age, prior to the end of MM IA, namely before 2000 B.C.

The Tholos Tomb B building complex was most probably used for the burial and worship of royalty up to the LM IIIA period (first half of the 14th century B.C.), and thus saw continuous use for more than six hundred years. It is natural that successive additions and modifications of scale should have been made over this long time span, eventually arriving at a large externally rectangular building complex with the tholos inscribed almost within the centre. At some points the complex was two-storied with a stairway leading to the upper floor; there was also a Pillar Crypt and other apartments. In many respects, this building – totaling 12 different areas – is a unique structure both in the Minoan and the Aegean world. Despite the constant changes, however, its architectural unity was preserved: a rectangular complex with a tholos at the centre.

Chronologically, at least five different architectural phases can be discerned in the Tholos Tomb B building complex. A sixth may exist, while the earlier use of Funerary Building 7 is not included. Any attempt to follow the course of the building complex over its six hundred year history must rely not only on interpretation of the architecture, but also on examination of the dateable evidence found there. The periods discerned by the excavations are: MM IA (*ca.* 2100-2000 B.C.), MM II (*ca.* 1900-1700 B.C.), LM II (*ca.* 1450 B.C.) and LM IIIA (*ca.* 1400-1300 B.C.) Interestingly, the six building phases are dated to only three of these periods: MM IA, LM II and LM IIIA. Indeed, the first four building phases are dated to MM IA; the fifth to some time during another later period, but significantly relatively early, when the monument was consolidated to continue in use for hundreds of years. Lastly, the modifications made during the sixth building phase are attributed to LM IIIA.

Any description, or even comprehension, of the architectural phases in their entirety is difficult for such a complicated monument. Therefore it has been deemed preferable to describe each area individually in the synoptic report below.

The tomb's dromos – **Area 1** – was downhill and constructed with a double wall. The inner wall of the tholos itself was lower, evidently to support the roof, part of which was preserved at the tholos entrance. In its initial form, the dromos must have been smaller.

During the sixth building phase (LM IIIA), the dromos was blocked at three places: one adjacent to the outside wall of the tholos with masonry perfectly imitating that of the older structure, and two within the dromos with very rough stone masonry. Between these barriers (which were re-

65

65. Aerial photograph of the central part of the Phourni cemetery. Tholos Tomb B to the right.

66. Ground plan of Tholos Tomb B and Funerary Building 7.

66

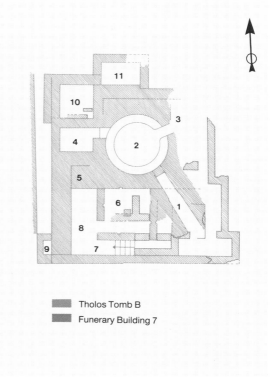

Tholos Tomb B
Funerary Building 7

moved during the excavations) canine remains came to light at many points. In some cases almost the entire skeleton of these animals was preserved, while in others the head had been removed from the body. The custom of beheading sacrifices is also encountered in the example of the bull's head from Tholos Tomb A. Moreover, dog sacrifices are known from Dendra. This Mycenaean predilection for animal sacrifice was even encountered in the area beneath the inner barrier where pig, dog, and rabbit bones as well as wild boar tusks came to light, no doubt remnants of sacrifices. Even parts of clay Horns of Consecration were found here, along with crab pincers.

Area 2, the tholos proper, was built with circular layers of large hewn blocks with especial care shown in the construction of the antae at the entrance and in the opening into Area 4 (the western side-chamber). The lintel consists of a huge block that follows the incline of the vaulting on the inside.

Finds from a trench made at the entrance attributed the initial construction of the tholos to the first building phase in the MM IA period. Furthermore, the tholos constituted the original core of the complex. However, the use of this tholos from the first building phase up to the sixth and last in LM IIIA is unknown. Dated to the latter period is the raising of the floor, the obstruction of the original entrance and that to Area 4, the construction of the bench, and the opening of a new entrance to Area 3.

The raising of the tholos floor was not achieved by a simple fill of earth but through a more complicated process. Large stone slabs were placed in successive interconnecting layers. A covering of clay and earth was applied to the last of these layers to create a flat surface; at some points of this floor, however, the stone slabs were still visible.

After the raising of the floor, a bench was built running completely around the circular tholos wall, with the exception of a space in front of the entrance to Area 3. At this point, the ends of the bench are neatly finished thus indicting that it was

67. Agate seal-stone depicting a cow suckling her calf, from Tholos Tomb B.

67

constructed at the same time as the opening of the entrance. The bench also traversed the tomb's blocked front entrance, but was removed hence when the trench was dug during the recent excavations.

The blocking of the doorway to Area 4, as with that of the tholos' original outer entrance, was made with large stones hewn in imitation of the original tholos masonry. This imitation was so successful, indeed, that one cannot help but call to mind Herodotus' narration about the similar concealment technique used by Hyrieus.

Lastly, during this same sixth building phase a new entrance was opened to the north-east from Area 3, utterly necessary now if the tholos was to be entered. It is noteworthy, however, that when compared with the other modifications mentioned above this entrance was quite roughly constructed.

Unfortunately, the finds from the tholos did not throw light upon the long use of this so important part of the complex. The spherical clay loom weight which was uncovered, and whose presence was puzzling until other such objects were found in the immediately adjacent Building 4, is typical of the disruption encountered in this section. However, the LM IIIA modifications could only have been made to facilitate ritual practices within the complex. A characteristic example of such rituals is provided by the terracotta models found in the Kamilari tholos tomb, one of which depicts a ritual dance within a circular structure, while the other shows the dead sitting upright awaiting the offerings of the living.

More interesting were the finds from a small trench immediately in front of the blocked entrance to the dromos and under the LM IIIA bench. At this point, and underneath the successive layers of stone slabs mentioned above, a MM IA bell-shaped figurine was found together with a few human bones and teeth, some animal bones, a boar's tusk, part of a small tripod vase, parts of a large steatite jar and of a bird's nest vase, also of steatite, an obsidian blade, and a gold band folded in two.

Area 3, the eastern side-chamber, was extensively destroyed but its existence is certain since the tholos wall is abruptly interrupted at the northeast corner and a frontage is created for a wall with a north-south orientation. The excavations here gave up only a clay votive foot, a spherical amethyst bead, another of greenstone, and fragments of an obsidian blade.

Area 4, the western side-chamber, is the best preserved section of Tholos Tomb B. On ground plan it is rectangular with a small dromos leading from the tholos. Its foundations are higher than those of the tholos due to the rising ground level and it is typical that a large mass of natural rock should have been left untouched in its western section. The north and south walls are vertical up to a certain point where they begin abruptly to incline towards the centre, thus forming a saddle roof of which not a few antefix slabs are preserved. A thick layer of plaster covered the walls of Area 4 including the blocked up entrance to Area 5 in the south wall, which – once again – imitated the masonry of the main wall.

Area 4 must have been constructed during the complex's first building phase. The nature of its use is unknown, however, until the sixth and last LM IIIA building phase to which remnants of a robbed burial or burials in the chamber are attributed. It is certain, however, that the area was blocked off from the tholos during the last building phase.

68. Gold ring with a depiction of the goddess with a griffin. From Tholos Tomb B.

Along with many human bone fragments, the excavations uncovered a host of broken pieces of ivory which must have belonged to various objects: amongst these were three small columns and a small fragment from a duck turning its head. Other finds from the robbed LM IIIA burials include two seal-stones, one of agate depicting a suckling cow and the other of sard showing two bulls. There is no doubt that these small finds belong to an important robbed burial or burials, perhaps royal. This is, of course, an important indication for the use not only of Area 4 but of the whole building complex of Tholos Tomb B.

Area 5, the south-west side-chamber, is preserved in a markedly good condition. The very thick construction of the chamber's three walls (north, east and west) and even its roof of successive stone slabs reminiscent of those covering the raised tholos floor mentioned above, contributed not only to the area's preservation but also to its safe concealment. Investigation of the chamber roof revealed significant traces of a second storey: a wall running east to west and a second going north to south meeting each other at a right angle. As we shall see in the description of Area 8, this section of the second floor was approached by a stairway from the south.

A crypt had been constructed under the preserved roof of Area 5. A chest larnax had been placed along the west wall at a relatively high level and was concealed by loose rubble walls to the south and east. Due to the constricted nature of the space it would have been impossible to wedge the larnax into place after the walls had been built and thus, undoubtedly, the opposite process was followed. In the narrow area between the outer walls of the larnax and the crypt only an ornately decorated steatite bead was found.

This attempt to conceal a larnax, exceptional even by the standards of Phourni where a rich variety of burial customs are attested, is not paralleled anywhere in Minoan Crete. However, it is explained by the larnax itself which, contrary to expectations, was not used for a single burial but as an ossuary for many.

The ossuary was full to the top with the remains of no less than 19 people. Since the lid of the larnax had remained sealed and airtight for many centuries the bones were found exactly in the position they had been laid and it was easy to discern not only parts of the skull and femoral bones, but also phalanges of the hand and sacra bones which till now have never been preserved even in undisturbed burials either in Phourni or in other graves in Crete. Mention should also be made of the bright red colour of the bones at the moment of their discovery, as if they had been washed in wine, as well as the fact that they had clearly been divided into categories. On the base of the larnax to the north, and underneath layers of various smaller bones, femoral fragments had been placed one above the other, while skulls had been similarly positioned along the south wall.

Once again, we are presented with an important anthropological find. Study of the bones indicated that the remains were those of at least 19 persons. One was a child at least 5 years of age, another slightly older. Three persons were between 17 and 25, seven between 25 and 35 and one between 33 and 45. The other six persons had lost their teeth prior to death and thus no calculation of their age was possible. Sex was not established

for all persons but at least six men and five women were identified. Of great importance was information on height calculated from the femoral bone which is rarely fully preserved even in undisturbed burials. Five persons were higher that 1.70m. (namely 1.7058, 1.7225, 1.7341 and 1.7457m.) One person measured 1.7636m., extremely high for his time. Pathological examination showed that apart from those who had lost their teeth, some of the dead suffered from osteoarthritis. One clavicula bore traces of a «meatus fracture» and a sacrum bone had a related anomaly due to spina bifida.

In addition to the anthropological information, the archaeological data provided by this unique find are naturally also of interest. For here we have a significant case of veneration of the dead in Minoan Crete, the ramifications of which are great – especially when one considers that amongst the human bones a few animal remains were also found (bovine, sheep, pig and hare). A Late Minoan IIA jug was used for a funerary libation during the concealment of the larnax, thus providing an important indication for the dating of this sealed find.

Area 6, the Pillar Crypt, is without doubt the most important area in the Tholos Tomb B building complex after the tholos itself. Fortunately, it is in a good state of preservation with its fill deposits undisturbed.

When compared with other rooms of Tholos Tomb B, and even with other structures in the cemetery as a whole, the room's carefully constructed masonry is noteworthy in that all four walls have sockets for the insertion of perpendicular wooden beams.

A doorway communicating with Area 8 (the western part of the stairway) exists in the southern part of the room's west wall, which at the same time represents the only access to Area 6. The same doorway must have provided access for both Areas 6 and 8 with the upper story since its antae were preserved to a level somewhat higher than that of both areas' upper floor. An interesting architectural peculiarity in the Pillar Crypt's south party-wall with the southern part of the stairway (Area 7) is a small (and luckily well preserved) rectangular opening in the lower eastern section of the wall. The wall itself continues regularly above the opening and no doubt would have been supported at that point by a wooden beam.

The Pillar Crypt was constructed during the second building phase in the MM IA period, as an extension to the pre-existing, and until then outer, tholos wall. It is certain that this room, being a basic component of Tholos Tomb B, continued in use without interruption throughout all the successive periods right up to and including LM IIIA. Sherds found in the room's undisturbed fill helped date the later building phases to MM II, MM III, and LM IA, even though this fill was partly created by the collapse of the room on the upper storey.

The room above Area 6 must have had a funerary function since the fill deposits included many small pieces of human bone and teeth as well as skull fragments. Various fragmentary finds indicate that the burials must have been richly endowed with offerings.

The most important object from Tholos Tomb B was found close to a crumpled leaf of gold in the area between the pillar and the west wall, where the number of bones was greatest: a gold ring depicting the goddess with a griffin. A unique steatite ring in the shape of a bull's head was uncovered between the pillar and the east wall. The remaining finds included a large cylindrical clay vase, a plain conical cup and a tripod vessel with handles. Another unique find, probably a funerary offering fallen from the upper floor, was a silver pin with a carved Linear A inscription. Finally, at the bottom part of the beam socket on the north wall, two large plain conical cups were found of which one had a crude spout and two perforated nipple-like protuberances.

The fill of the Pillar Crypt was throughout full of tiny fragments of fine plaster. Most of these were white, but not a few were coloured black, yellow, orange, red and blue. Despite the mass of fragments, their almost microscopic size did not permit their reassembly to discover some motif or depiction. Only two fragments were found with clear traces of decoration: black papyrus motifs on an orange ground, perhaps part of a scene depicting ornate garments. Many fragments preserve a combination of two or three colours. There is little doubt that most of these belonged to frescoes which covered the Pillar Crypt's walls, something which would be quite unusual for a funerary building. Moreover, Pillar Crypts were not simple chambers but, as we know from Minoan architecture, were determined for cult use.

Area 7, the southern part of the stairway, is the most difficult area of the complex to make sense of since its floor is no longer visible due to the deep excavations made in the older Funerary Building 7. Area 7 was a passageway going east to west with various openings to the north and five steps almost in the centre. Its western section

led to the higher level of Area 8. Area 7 is the main approach to the south-west part of the complex and the second floor. It is almost certain that entry to the Area would have been made from the east, as is the case with nearly all the buildings in the cemetery.

The eastern section of the south wall was built just on top of the south wall of the old Funerary Building 7. Of some importance is the visible distinction which can be readily made between each of these walls just opposite from Area 1 (the tomb's dromos). At that point the newer wall is discerned from the older not only by its masonry but also by the slight difference in its orientation and, of course, in the newer foundation level which is clearly apparent. This level is the same as that of the base of the first step from the east; in other words, the new wall is on the same level as the corridor of Area 7. At the same time, however, this also marks the foundation level of the west wall of Area 1. Thus it is certain that the construction of the stairway is contemporary to that of Area 1.

The distinguishable masonry of Area 7's south wall consists of well-worked blocks surrounded by many smaller stones in a particularly attractive manner. This masonry is quite important since its construction can be associated chronologically with that of other walls in the building complex. Precisely the same masonry technique is employed in the construction of the south wall of Area 12 which, however, constitutes an outer addition to the original tholos wall. Indeed, at the north-west corner of the south wall of Area 11 one can clearly discern that it was constructed prior to two other walls subsequently added alongside it, and for this reason the older wall was attributed to the fourth building stage of the complex. Thus the south wall of Area 7, due to the similarity of its peculiar masonry, undoubtedly belongs to the same fourth building phase and, consequently, so do all the other areas which surround it.

Area 8, the western section of the stairway at the south-west corner of the Tholos Tomb B building complex, is only approachable from Area 7, and is elongated, although slightly wider than Area 7. On turning a corner it leads north and, by means of another stairway, to the second floor. This area is at a level corresponding to the height of the last step of Area 7.

Fortunately, some important evidence for the function of Area 8 was preserved in the west wall while more came to light during excavations. The inner face of the west wall contained small openings at a regular height and distance which could only have been used as sockets for wooden beams to take a stairway. The excavations uncovered the lower monolithic, slab-like steps of this stairway to the north although they were subsequently removed due to their much damaged condition, as well as to facilitate the examination of Area 5. Significantly, the width of the stairway did not extend across the entire width of the corridor (Area 8) but only across part of it to the west. This no doubt facilitated access to the ground floor Pillar Crypt as well as to Area 5. A spherical amethyst bead, two gold cut-outs, two pieces of ivory, part of a rock-crystal inlay, and a fragment of a steatite vase were found during the excavation of the Area.

Area 9, the independent south-west side-chamber, was built onto the outer south-west corner of the Tholos Tomb B building complex. At least three surface burials were made there with funerary offerings of an ivory seal bearing hieroglyphics, and an amulet.

Area 10, the north-west side-chamber, contained a disturbed burial near the south wall. The body had been placed on its right side in a foetus position. A lentoid steatite seal-stone with linear motifs was found between the finger bones.

Finally, in **Area 11**, the northern side-chamber, two burials had taken place in two layers, on top of which many fragments of stone vases were found amongst a host of fallen stones from the northern part of the Tholos Tomb B complex. In the upper burial layer, a chest larnax placed along the south wall in the south-west corner was found to contain the remains of two bodies. The lower burial layer had surface graves with funerary offerings of ivory seals and MM IA cups. The early date of these burials in this attached room is important for the early dating of the entire Tholos Tomb B building complex.

There is no doubt that Tholos Tomb B was the most important funerary monument at Phourni, and one of the most significant of all those in Crete. This is clear from its use for so many centuries for the burial and veneration of even royal personages.

Funerary Building 7

Funerary Building 7, used for burials and deposits of remains in the MM IA period (*ca.* 2100-2000 B.C.), was one of the most important Prepalatial buildings of the cemetery judging from its central position, its construction and the finds which came to light there. The building is, however, poorly preserved due to the fact that Tholos Tomb B was erected on top of it. Funerary Building 7 consists of at least six rooms some of whose floors were paved. In relation to Tholos Tomb B, two of these rooms are underneath the eastern part of the Pillar Crypt, another two under the area just in front of the stairway, a fifth to the east of the dromos and the sixth underneath the south-west side-chamber.

The rooms uncovered from beneath the later Pillar Crypt of Tholos Tomb B were the most disturbed. Found amongst scattered bones in the northern room was part of a faience scarab, stone vase fragments, obsidian blades, a few sea shells and two small pieces of gold cut-out. The southern paved room contained the remains of one person in a foetus position, and a steatite seal-stone.

More important finds were made in the two rooms underneath the area in front of the later stairway of Tholos Tomb B. In the western room, deposits of skulls and skeletons were made at surface level. A total of six skulls were found; funerary offerings accompanying the dead included two miniature clay vases, part of a stone jar, a bronze pair of tweezers, 61 beads from two necklaces, and sea shells. Also of interest were three seals found in the same room together with a clay sealing depicting an animal, possibly an imprint of a three-sided prism seal. A most significant find for the minor plastic arts in Minoan Crete (especially when Cycladic and other Eastern influences are considered) is the stone figurine of a standing male with his hands below the breast.

The eastern room in front of the Tholos Tomb B stairway was undisturbed. The burial layer consisted of six larnakes, together with bone deposits on the paved floor. The larnakes contained a total of 14 skulls. Another 15 skulls were found in the open spaces between them, especially to the north-east. Funerary offerings included a bronze dagger, a handleless cup, many sea shells, part of an obsidian blade, a necklace with eleven beads of sard and rock crystal, and four seals. The latter included a cylinder seal bearing a depiction of humans, lions and birds, while a second in the shape of a seated animal bore a representation of three scorpions. A clay vase found inside one of the larnakes was especially interesting: a LM single-handled kylix, hundreds of years younger than the larnax or the room's burials. This must have been deposited during a libation, yet another indication of tomb cult, made when this section of the later corridor in Tholos Tomb B was constructed.

The burial layer of the fifth room of Funerary Building 7, located to the east of the later dromos of Tholos Tomb B, consisted of a deposit in the doorway which communicated with the previous room, and an interesting burial along the length of the east wall in the area to the south. The body here had been placed in a foetus position. Of the skull, only the jaw was in its original position with a plain conical cup underneath it. The rest of the skull had been separated from the body and was found upside-down near the legs, once again with an upturned plain conical cup on the top. Found near the remains was the bottom part of a large vase with plaster both inside and out, and, most importantly, a unique bronze statuette with its hands resting below the breast. Finally, uncovered along the length of the wall were three small round gold cut-outs which evidently served as the trimmings for some object. Six plain conical cups came to light in various parts of the room.

The sixth room of Funerary Building 7 is located exactly under the Crypt and north-west side-chamber of Tholos Tomb B. Preserved here was a section of a wall and part of the paved floor on which bone deposits had also been made. A skull with two gold cut-outs was found on the paved floor nearby together with a thin gold band, a sea shell and an ivory pyramidal seal. Funerary Building 7, finally, must have also included that layer of burial deposit found in the southern part of the west wing of the Tholos Tomb B stairway. 15 skulls had been deposited here on the natural rock together with many bones. Funerary offerings included a disc-like whorl, four spherical amethyst beads, a plain conical cup, 16 sea shells of which two were perforated, and a wild-boar tusk.

69

70

69. *Egyptian faience scarabs: above, from Funerary Building 7; below, from Funerary Building 6.*

70. *Ivory zoomorphic seal, from Funerary Building 7.*

71. Bronze figurine, from Funerary Building 7.

Funerary Building 6 and the surrounding area

Of all the funerary buildings in the Phourni cemetery made so complicated by continuous use and the various modifications and additions, Funerary Building 6 is perhaps the simplest example of an ossuary. Located to the west of Tholos Tomb B and north of Funerary Buildings 5 and 12, it was built onto naked rock during the MM 1A period (ca. 2000 B.C.) at the highest part of the cemetery. The building is significant not only because of its finds but also since it was surrounded by roads, paved areas and even a stairway from which certain ritual acts were performed involving, as we shall see, the casting down of vases and other vessels.

Of the six rooms in Funerary Building 6, four elongated rooms running north to south were in a good condition and it is clear that they were added, one parallel to the other, each time an increase in burial space was needed. The fact that

some of these have no door indicates that communication was made from above by means of a stairway from the wooden roof, a feature not uncommon in other buildings of the cemetery. The rooms could not have had high ceilings.

Dense deposits of skull and bone as well as burials were initially made on the floors of the rooms and only later in larnakes, pithoi and vases. The density of skull deposits in relatively cramped areas is typical, such as in the two eastern rooms where a total of 196 skulls were deposited. A few larnakes had been placed one inside the other. There is no doubt that the deposits were made after clearing of neighbouring funerary buildings, and indeed of tholos tombs. In Funerary Building 6 in particular, the finding of skulls without other bones was clearly evident. A characteristic case is the skull found inside a vase. Equally worthy of note is that the lower jaw was in many cases missing as it had no doubt fallen away after decomposition of the flesh. Finally, a few pieces of plaster were found in the fill of the rooms – and indeed inside one skull. This, as far as burial custom is concerned, is reminiscent of the coating of skulls with plaster known in the East. The few animal bones and teeth found may be the remnants of funerary meals or offerings to the dead –30 sea shells for instance were uncovered here.

Many of the shell deposits and the burials made in Funerary Building 6 were accompanied by rich offerings. More than 70 clay vases of various shapes were found (mostly small jugs, plain conical cups, bowls, single-handled cylindrical or globular cups and pyxides) which perhaps contained offerings for the dead. The same applies to two stone vases: a bird's nest vase of white-veined black stone, and a jug. In one room two bell-shaped figurines were even found; in others, two bronze cutters, no doubt used as tools during life and now accompanying their owners to the other world.

Many pieces of jewelery accompanied the burials or the deposits: a bronze pin, two necklaces with stone beads (one of which may have suspended a bronze ring as an amulet) and quite a few ivory and bone amulets, as well as one of gold made from a triangular gold cut-out with a

72. Steatite figurine, from Funerary Building 7.

73. Larnax from Funerary Building 6.

suspension hole at the top. A unique ivory amulet has the shape of a pregnant woman, and another is decorated with two plastic animal heads.

The most important finds here, however, are the 16 seals, most of which are made of ivory (with a few of steatite) and in a variety of shapes (conical, cylindrical, discoid, three-sided prism, button, pyramidal, circular pyramidal and stepped pyramidal); some theriomorphic examples also exist. Unique amongst these is an elongated parallel-sided seal with a total of 14 sealing surfaces and a suspension hole in its cylindrical terminal for use as an amulet. In their entirety the seals from Funerary Building 6 bear a variety of scenes: human figures and animals, vegetal and geometric motifs, mostly in the torsional shapes characteristic of the period. One of the seals depicts three seated human figures and is framed around the edges with a torsional two-lobe motif. A more characteristic example of such motifs can be found in another seal with four goats whose horns inter-link in the centre to form a cross with circles in the spaces between the cross-arms. One hollow

cylinder seal is closed at each end by a thick disc of ivory; it may have once held some apotropeic substance and was thus kept as an amulet. Another unique ivory seal was fashioned in the shape of a fly. It is not impossible that some symbolism is hidden here since Homer compares the audacity of the fly with the valour of his heroes. The fly, moreover, symbolised courage in Egypt and for this reason medallions were awarded bearing its image. Finally, of exceptional importance is the group of hieroglyphic seals, some of the oldest well-dated examples of script in Minoan Crete. All the above seals from Funerary Building 6 are truly exceptional and, together with other seals from Phourni, go to confirm the existence of an early seal-glyptic workshop at Archanes.

The funerary offerings mentioned here, in particular the seals (and especially the ivory specimens), underline the important position held by those buried in Funerary Building 6. Note also that a few larnakes in the building bore incised traces of script, not especially rare elsewhere at Phourni but most exceptional for Minoan Crete as a whole. The many instances of script dating from the first years of the cemetery's use can only go to betray developed trading activity by the settlement's in-

74

74. Selection of pottery from the deposit of Funerary Building 6.

habitants. This is clearly borne out by the Egyptian faience scarab also found in Funerary Building 6, as well as by the wealth of offerings, which is even more convincing evidence for trade than the lavish use of ivory. In this respect, mention can be made of another early and important piece of ivory work, a thick plaque with a griffin carved on one side. Perhaps the importance of the burials and deposits in Funerary Building 6 necessitated that this more than any other building should have been set apart by the creation of approaches, and even of a paved surface and stairways for the performance of certain ritual ceremonies, discussed below.

An uphill stepped road paved with large slabs leads to Funerary Building 6 from the lower level of the hill immediately to the east, passing parallel to Tholos Tomb B to the north. Found north of this road were about 20 vases (some inside another) which may have been buried as offerings to the dead. Extending southwards is an elongated passage which proved to be the site of other more significant finds.

This blind passage divides the lower level of Tholos Tomb B from the higher one of Funerary Building 6 by means of a sturdy curtain-wall some

3m. high. The passage was clearly not used as a thoroughfare since the rock surface therein was left in its natural state. The western curtain-wall, which defines the passage, was constructed with the single purpose of retaining the earth around the higher Funerary Building 6, and more particularly the paved surface created along the eastern side of that building. This paved surface also contained sporadic deposits of a few vases as well as an interesting terracotta figurine of a male holding his hands below the breast. These finds are associated with ritual acts which took place in the passage from the vantage point of the paved area, and more specifically from a three-stepped stairway at the north end of the passage.

From the height of the paved area and the position on the steps some 300 vases had been thrown east into the blind passage. These vases were found in a large pile, but in distinguishable groups, with pure earth between them indicating that not one, but a succession of deposits was made over time. This is the most important such

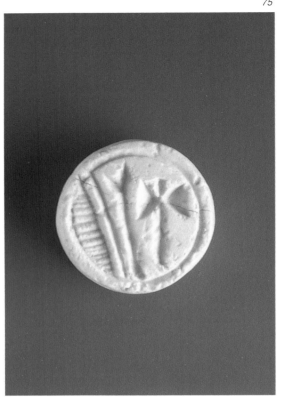

burial deposit in Minoan Crete and includes a large selection of known (and not a few up till now unknown) pottery types ranging in size from miniature to large. The vases bear dark on light and light on dark decoration, but some are polychrome and in a few cases even plastic relief ornamentation is used. All together, they are most important for the study of the early stages of Minoan pottery. All the known types of cup are encountered: plain conical ring-based, one-handled cylindrical, carinated bowls, globular beak-spouted jugs, tripodal vases, two-handled bridge- spouted jars, strainers, and kernoi. Of special interest is a large kernos consisting of a tall, cylindrical, perforated base on which three interconnecting globular vases were set, two of them closed and the other open, and all three decorated with barbotine plastic ornaments reminiscent of cactus plants. The vessel had a high cylindrical handle. The openings made in the walls of the vessel's base are noteworthy since they are in the shape of ritual motifs: Horns of Consecration, double axes and incurved altars.

Notable by their absence in the Archanes dump are common domestic vessels of the period – even in fragmentary form – and larger vases and utensils, pithoi and larnakes. The dump's contents cannot thus have come from the clearing of funerary buildings. Also missing are the small objects typical of clearing remains, such as bones. Only one bronze cutter was found in the blind passage, but to the north of the dump. For this reason the deposit can only have had a ritual character as, in any case, the kernoi indicate. More indicative is yet another find, an animal skull – possibly that of a bull. This was found in the main deposit mentioned above, in the centre of the area behind and to the west of the side-chamber of Tholos Tomb B. Certain other ritual acts, however, took place at other points in the passageway where other important pottery deposits came to light. To the north, a clay terracotta figurine of an adorant was found, and to the south quite a few animal

Ivory seals from Funerary Building 6: 75. With hieroglyphics, 76. Fly-shaped, 77. With a torsional depiction of three seated human figures in the centre, 78. Torsional representation of four wild goats, 79. Unique four-sided seal with hieroglyphic and figural representations.

jaw bones with their teeth intact, once again remnants of a sacrifice.

It is clear that these ritual ceremonies occurred after the erection of Funerary Building 6 since the structures referred to (the uphill dromos, the curtain-wall, and the paved area) were all constructed after the erection of the building and certainly before the development of the west wall of Tholos Tomb B. The importance of these well cared-for structures in the operation of the cemetery can be seen from the clay pipes found in the passage which were once located on the upper paved area, no doubt to channel away libations. The care taken in the maintenance of these buildings in this part of the cemetery is further highlighted by the positioning of large, rectangular, upright stone slabs along the length of the outer western wall of Tholos Tomb B and at its foundations to protect the building against water.

FUNERARY BUILDINGS 12, 5, 3, AND 8

Just as Funerary Building 6 is characterised by its architectural simplicity, so the funerary buildings erected just to the south of it are notable for their complexity. This is mostly due to the fact that this area was intensively used for hundreds of years with, as we shall see, the demolition of walls and erection of new buildings on their remains. Study of the area, which was not simply limited to architectural remains, indicated that the first building of this group to be constructed was Funerary Building 25 which lies under the following structure, the large Funerary Building 5. Following this in order come Funerary Buildings 12, 3 and 8. Funerary Building 26 (of which very few remains have come to light) was certainly built prior to Funerary Building 8, although it is not known precisely when in relation to the building phases of the other structures.

Funerary Building 12

Funerary Building 12 is only modestly preserved and thus no accurate appraisal can be made of its architectural form. The only features ascertained with certainty are two elongated rooms, one to the north running from east to west, and another to the west going from south to north. It is certain, however, from the nature of the site, the finds and especially from the paved areas to the east, that this building was an ossuary with compartments one next to the other, and similar

to neighbouring Funerary Building 6 discussed above.

Just as with Funerary Building 6, so Funerary Building 12 contained skull deposits from the clearing of other funerary buildings. Sporadic deposits were found at various points, in two cases with 15 and 20 skulls respectively placed on the ground with, once again, very few other bones. The funerary offerings accompanying these skulls were similar to those found in Funerary Building 6: clay pots and a few stone vases, a whetstone, a pestle, obsidian blades, a few steatite beads, some bone amulets, an ivory three-sided prism seal, and four smaller gold objects.

The deposited remains of Funerary Building 12, even though not well preserved, seem nevertheless to have been important since new offerings were made with them on their reinterment, as we can see from the a few animal bones and sea shells. Their significance is confirmed by the paved areas discovered to the east (similar to those of Funerary Building 6), and even by the open space left as a kind of dais between the Tholos Tomb B, Funerary Building 3 and Funerary Building 5.

This area was used during at least three different periods. At the end of the EM period, the first paved area was constructed. In the following MM IA period, the whole area was covered with yellow earth. And during a third phase at the beginning of the MM period, another paved surface was laid. These areas, apart from their connection with various funerary buildings, may at this point have served some ritual function, a hypothesis confirmed by the finds. On one of these, about 20 vases were found, including both cups and jugs. At the same point, a sea shell was found together with fragments of an animal skull; remnants of some sacrifice. The similar function of these paved areas with the corresponding area in neighbouring Funerary Building 6 is also clear from the clay water-pipes found fallen (probably from here) in two rooms of neighbouring Funerary Building 5.

Funerary Building 5

Funerary Building 5 which is dated to the MM

80. Ornate clay ritual kernos, from the deposit of Funerary Building 6.

IA period (before 2000 B.C.) is one of the largest in Phourni. It was built on top of Funerary Building 25 but its entire south-west section was destroyed with the erection of Funerary Building 3. Funerary Building 5 preserves a total of ten rooms constructed in wings during various building phases; some of these have no communicating doorways. The central part of the building has six rooms in two parallel groups, the west wing has one room, and the east wing to the south of Funerary Building 3 another three. The central section was the first to be built while the two wings constitute additions.

The main use made of Funerary Building 5 was for surface burials in larnakes or pithoi, and skull deposits – in many cases in successive layers. The single room of the west wing contained burials and deposits in 21 pithoi and two larnakes. The pithoi contained one to four burials each, while ten skulls were found in one of the larnakes. The funerary offerings found in the room included a bronze pin, an amulet made from a tusk, beads of gold, amethyst and sard, and a singular lapis lazuli cylinder seal imported from the East depicting a male figure. Of the funerary offerings found in the central part of the building, mention may be made of an ivory amulet in the form of a double-headed bird.

The construction of a small square room to the south-east of the central wing of the building and south-west of Funerary Building 3 warrants interest for the false door therein, of which both the antae and the lintel are preserved. The door's deceptive nature is confirmed not only by its small dimensions but also by the fact that the deposits and burials reached the height of its lintel, thus indicating that they could only have been made from the roof above. Schist slabs may have been employed in the rooves of some of the rooms since a few such fragments were found fallen therein.

The two burial layers excavated in this room provided interesting information on burial customs of the period. A great number of deposits and burials were made from the roof, including child-burials in vases. A total of 37 skulls were found along with many bones. Many of the skull deposits were made onto slab-like stones, while others were placed in vases. These were accompanied by about 20 vases, conical and carinated cups, bridge-spouted jars, jugs an so on.

The eastern rooms of Funerary Building 5 to the south of Funerary Building 3 were utilised in two phases, the more recent of which demolished the partition wall to create one integrated space. During the earlier phase, the dead were laid directly onto the ground surface in the larger western room, together with child- burials in vases. In the south-west part of this room, depositions of pottery had also been made. Over 70 vases were found here as well as conical cups, bowls, bridge-spouted jars, jugs, a few miniature vases, and even two seals, one of ivory and another (very rare for Minoan Crete) of lead. In the small east room of the older phase, burials and deposits had taken place both on the surface and in two larnakes containing two burials each with interesting funerary offerings such as two seals bearing depictions of scorpions. It was here that a find unique for Phourni was made: a stippled bull rhyton. Finally, during the later phase and in the now unified room, burials in five larnakes and in two pithoi were made together with deposits of 31 skulls on the ground accompanied by funerary goods including an ivory dagger handle and a three- sided steatite prism seal.

In comparison with the ossuaries described above, the chronologically later Funerary Building 5 is interesting not only for the new evidence it provides but more so for the individualization of the burials apparent in the regular arrangement of pithoi and larnakes, even though they usually contain more than one burial. Instances of food offerings are now limited, animal bones and sea shells being only sporadically encountered. Perhaps the great amount of pottery indicates that libations were now more frequent. Respect for the dead previously interred in the building had not declined, however, since the older burials were in no way disturbed despite the destruction visited on the building and the erection of the imposing Funerary Building 3.

Funerary Building 3

Funerary Building 3, rich in finds and significant for its individual burials, is exceptionally interesting for its architectural form in that it belongs to a type new to Phourni. It consists of a square and extremely well-built symmetrical structure in a markedly fine state of preservation and with a total of six rooms. The five building phases identified here failed to alter the building's overall architectural unity.

The two parallel rectangular rooms to the west were the first to be built. Their doorways, facing east, and finely worked antae and thresholds no

81

81. Eastern cylinder seal made of lapis lazuli, together with a reconstructed drawing of the full scene depicted thereon. From Funerary Building 5.

82. Agate seal-stone with a depiction of a bull. From Funerary Building 3.

doubt imitate domestic architecture of the period. To this main structure, the other rooms were later added to the east. The walls in the west rooms were recessed at a certain height, an interesting architectural feature which facilitated the support of joists for a wooden floor, namely an upper storey. The floor of this storey may have been covered with a layer of pebble and dash, remnants of which were found in the same building. Fragments of fallen schist slabs were also uncovered which must have come from the roof. In another building phase, small transverse walls were constructed in the original rooms, perhaps to delineate certain burials. The last architectural phase, however, saw the construction of a stairway of seven stone steps at the building's north-east corner. The lower part of this stairway formed a landing which turned and led to the interior.

The approach from above, noted in the older ossuaries at Phourni, now takes on a monumental form. For one to reach the height of the landing, an external wooden staircase was necessary which, in the building's final state, could only have been accommodated on the east side, at the north-east corner between Funerary Buildings 3 and 8. The site of Funerary Building 3 should not be overlooked, wedged as it is between three other surrounding Funerary Buildings and, indeed, by Funerary Building 5 which it had destroyed to a large extent. The relation of Funerary Building 3 to its neighbouring buildings determines, furthermore, the dating of building and reconstruction work not only on the structure's original core, but also on the additions. It is notable, nevertheless, that the burials which came to light here are not associated with the architectural phases of the building. Quite possibly, then, we have here an example of the clearing of funerary buildings of their original burials in order to receive others, the remnants of which were uncovered by the excavations.

In comparison with the older funerary buildings already described, Funerary Building 3 contained only a few burials in two layers in the north and west rooms; the south-west rooms were only used for access to the building. The burials of the upper layer must have been made in larnakes placed on the floor of the upper storey. They were found

disturbed and their exact number is unknown although they could not have been many. However, these would have been important burials judging by the extant funerary offerings which included an agate seal-stone with the depiction of a bull turning its head. Incised above the beast's body are three circles, while a triton appears below the belly.

The most important find from the upper burial level was a group of 25 different pieces of ivory which had once decorated a wooden artifact, or more than one; two of these pieces, however, were knife handles and another belonged to a comb. Four of the larger plaques were decorated with a relief lion shown in a «running gallop», while another even larger specimen portrays a scene unique in the Cretan-Mycenaean repertoire: a goat bending its head to gaze at a bush between its hooves. Funerary rites had been awarded the dead in the upper burial layer since fragments of four plaster tripod offering tables were found, one of

83. Ivory plaque with a depiction of a lion in a «flying gallop». From Funerary Building 3.

84. Ivory plaque with a depiction of a wild goat. From Funerary Building 3.

83

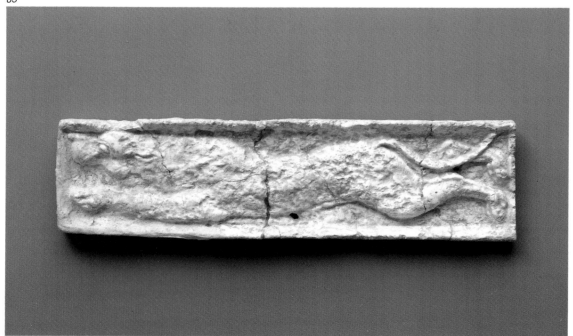

which was red and the other decorated with a yellow band.

The important burials from the lower burial layer had been made in four larnakes; two each in each of the two northern rooms. Significantly, the larnakes had not been placed on ground-level but were raised by means of some man-made fill. Both larnakes in the north-west room (which contained child burials) had been placed one next to the other in the north-west corner. Inside the northernmost was a gold ring, while underneath it was a small stone carinated vase (found upturned and containing a gold leaf), and a bronze lamp with a decorated handle. Next to the southern larnax, a unique globular diorite vase was found which may be an Early Dynasty Egyptian import older than the Minoan burial by many centuries.

The two other chest larnakes had been placed parallel to each other in the middle of the central room to the north. Found under the larnax to the south were fragments of a bronze vase and a gold cut-out in the shape of a figure-of-eight shield which no doubt once decorated some wooden object. Exceptional offerings had been placed underneath the larnax to the north: a silver cup,

85

three bronze weapons (a sword, a tongue-shaped knife, and a spearhead with a delicate, incised decoration of spirals, double pendants and foliate motifs.) Finally, and most importantly, a large rhyton made of Egyptian alabaster was uncovered, probably left here after the pouring of some libation.

The burials of the lower stratum in the two south rooms that were made on the ground were not well preserved, unlike those raised on man-made fill. But it is certain that at least two burials were made in the large west room, while the one found in the smaller central room to the south was accompanied by notable offerings. Found in the western room, apart from pieces of an obsidian blade, was an ivory comb whose shape is unique considering its early date. An ivory hieroglyphic seal was also uncovered. Burial offerings are suggested by an animal tooth and a few sea shells.

85. *Egyptian diorite vase. From Funerary Building 3.*

86. *Alabaster rhyton from Funerary Building 3.*

Few finds were made in the south central room.

The date of the finds from the south rooms (MM IA, i.e. before 2000 B.C.) make the associated burials the oldest in Funerary Building 3. The building was used for burials at least from this period and for centuries later up to the Postpalatial period (after 1400 B.C.) when the northern rooms were cleared and covered with earth to receive larnax burials. Gold beads from a necklace were found scattered throughout the south room up to the stairway and may originate from this clearing phase. The final burials were those of the upper burial stratum from the collapsed floor of the upper-storey.

The importance of both the early burials (which numbered at least three) with their hieroglyphic seals, and the later four in their respective larnakes, not to mention the disturbed burials from the upper storey, is well attested by their rich funerary offerings such as the silver cup and the Egyptian vase. Furthermore, the presence of a burial with three weapons – and fine specimens at that – is significant for Phourni. Finally, distinct traces of burial rites are apparent both in the early and later burials, although more pronounced in the latter with their offering tables and the unique alabaster rhyton.

Funerary Building 8

Funerary Building 8 is located east of 3 and north of 9. It was built on top of Funerary Building 29 whose foundations now appear as paving on the lowest level of the floor. This is a small rectangular building divided with a transverse wall into two elongated rooms which once communicated with each other by means of doorway to the south, later walled-up. A second corresponding wall was added to the building's west wall. It is not certain whether access to the building was made from the east wall or from above.

The surface deposit of Funerary Building 8 included, amongst other finds, a clay ball and a lentoid steatite seal-stone with a depiction of a

87. Bronze weapon from Funerary Building 3.

88. Gold necklace from Funerary Building 3.

89. Necklaces made of gold, glass paste and ivory. From Tholos Tomb C.

90. Gold ear pick from Funerary Building 8.

87

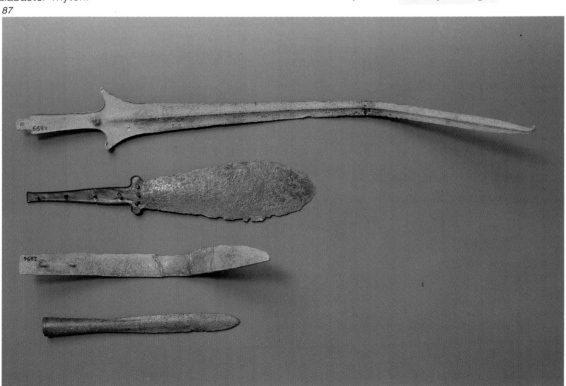

88

89

90

goat. While the eastern room is destroyed, there is little doubt that it was used for burials.

In the western room, burials had been made on the surface in two successive burial strata. The bottom of these contained 14 burials, twelve of which had been placed towards the north wall with the head close to or abutting a high built bench. A single funerary offering was found: a clay MM IA fruit bowl (before 2000 B.C.) In the upper burial level and in the south-west corner of the room, a burial delineated with stones was found with offerings of an upturned plain conical cup and a sea shell. The most important find from the building, however, came to light during the removal of material from the walled-up doorway between both rooms. This was a gold ear-pick, unique in Crete and comparable to relatively similar Mycenaean objects from a later period mostly found on mainland Greece.

THOLOS TOMB C AND FUNERARY BUILDINGS 9 AND 13

Tholos Tomb C was erected to the south and adjoins the eastern-most rooms of Funerary Building 5. To the east and south it abuts Funerary Building 9 under which lies the older Funerary Building 13. Finally, Building 22 with its scanty remains of a curved wall lies to the south-west of Tholos Tomb C.

Tholos Tomb C

Tholos Tomb C, built above ground level, is one of the best preserved Prepalatial tholos tombs in Crete. That it was vaulted is certain from the number and size of the stones used for the roof as well as from the inward direction with which they fell. The thick abutment walls of the rooms of Funerary Building 9 served as buttresses to support the tomb. Two double buttresses were, moreover, uncovered in the southern part of the tholos.

The low entrance to Tholos Tomb C faces east as is common in the tholos tombs of the Messara type. An important architectural peculiarity in this tholos tomb is the construction of a window just to the south of the entrance. Perhaps this window is associated with the adjacent construction of a Pi shaped hearth in the south-west part of the tholos.

An undisturbed single deposit level dated to the EM III period (ca. 2250-2100 B.C.) was found in Tholos Tomb C. Burials had taken place in eleven larnakes, all of them chests with the exception of one tub larnax, and a burial in a pithos placed in the centre of the tholos. Furthermore, deposits on ground level were found in the spaces between the larnakes, as well as at the entrance and in the dromos of the tholos. A total of 18 dead had been buried in the larnakes and the pithos, all in a foetus position. Most larnakes had only one burial, although the pithos and one larnax contained two each, and two other larnakes three each. 24 burials had been made between the larnakes indicated by a corresponding number of skulls; three more were found in the entrance. These burials no doubt took place after the deposition of the larnakes, especially those at the entrance, and in certain instances one body was buried on top of the other. All in all, 45 burials were made in Tholos Tomb C. This is the first time that a specific number of burials is known from a Prepalatial tholos tomb.

Funerary offerings were absent from the larnakes and the other surface burials. Only in the pithos were a few animal and fish bones and a sea shell found. On the other hand a large number of finds were uncovered underneath the larnakes accompanying the surface burials. The ground here had been covered by a thin layer of natural earth, now pinguid due to the disintegration of bodily substances. Immediately underneath this, the irregular ground surface of the tholos had been leveled with calcareous stones. All the funerary offerings from Tholos Tomb C were found in this layer of stones. The smaller objects were hidden amongst the stones while the bigger ones were protected between the larger stones which also helped support the larnakes. Most of the groups of offerings were found exactly underneath the larnakes, but also under the surface burials made around them.

An important number of finds came to light in Tholos Tomb C: a total of 269 items of which 164 were found under the larnakes and the pithos,

91. View from the west of Funerary Buildings 3 and 5 to the left and Tholos Tomb C to the right.

92. View of the larnakes of Tholos Tomb C during the excavations.

91

92

and 95 below the surface burials. It would not be possible to associate these finds with corresponding burials, even though for the first time it is possible to attribute specific finds to Prepalatial burials, an important event in statistical terms alone. However, it is necessary to mention a few according to type in order to provide some idea of the wealth and variety of the objects.

Only five clay vases were found in Tholos Tomb C. Noteworthy are the 80 sea shells found in a twin vase. To these vases must be added three stone examples: a Cycladic marble bowl and two others of steatite and schist. The eleven seals found were all made of ivory and not only indicate the social rank of the dead person but also constitute the only Minoan seals dated with certainty to this period. One of these bears a depiction of fish. Three bronze daggers were also found, the only Prepalatial examples found at Phourni.

A great range of jewelery was found in Tholos Tomb C made of a variety of materials (gold, silver, ivory, bone and faience) from which bands and circular sewn-on ornaments were made, as well as amulets, beads and even a gold cut-out in the shape of a foot. The amulets were cylindrical and drop-shaped. Two made of ivory were fish-shaped, and another depicted a bird. The gold beads used to adorn two necklaces (unique for Crete at this period) betray advanced techniques and, indeed, links with overseas. For not only is the valuable metal imported, but some of the distinctive ornate beads found here strongly resemble similar examples from the famous «Treasure of Priam» excavated by Schliemann at Troy.

Perhaps the most interesting group of finds is constituted by the figurines. Tholos Tomb C at Archanes gave up the richest group of figurines found in the Aegean, and not simply in Crete, including an important group of marble Cycladic figurines. A total of 15 figurines were found either intact, or in fragments belonging to separate

93. Heads from marble Cycladic figurines. From Tholos Tomb C.

94. Unique ivory Cycladic figurine. From Tholos Tomb C.

93

figurines. These were not only made of marble but also of other materials common in Crete and thus available at Archanes (ivory, schist, and even quartz). All are in their own special way unique. The most important is an ivory upright woman with an incision at the pubic triangle. The rendition of this figurine is so typical of Cycladic workmanship that it could not but have been made by a Cycladic craftsman.

Although Cycladic figurines have been found sporadically elsewhere in Crete, the twelve imported Cycladic figurines from Tholos Tomb C constitute the largest single such find ever made on the island and cover all the well-known Cycladic figurine types. The majority are in fragments, mostly feet, but one torso exists along with three heads with a fine plastic rendition of the mouth. The figurines' fragmentary nature would suggest that they were purposely broken when given as offerings during tomb cult rituals. Only two intact Cycladic figurines were found in Tholos Tomb C, not in the burial strata, however, but hidden in the tomb's wall. So many are the Cycladic figurines here that, together with the typically Cycladic nature of other offerings in the tomb and (as we shall see below) in the neighbouring Area of the Rocks, they manifest a pronounced Cycladic presence at Archanes which should in no way be ignored.

The 25 Cycladic figurines found in Tholos Tomb C, the Area of the Rocks to the south-west, and to the south, are far more than the total recovered from the rest of Crete. Apart from the undoubtedly imported Cycladic marble figurines and the bowls, certain materials such as silver and lead (found in Tholos Tomb C and neighbouring buildings) must also have been brought from the Cyclades. Obsidian was obviously another import and, indeed, its presence at Phourni is far from sporadic. 55 obsidian blades were found in Tholos Tomb B and over a thousand in the Area of the Rocks. A few more objects also have typological similarities with the Cyclades, such as the daggers and some of the amulets. Finally, ivory and bronze pins, uncommon in Crete and useless on the light Minoan loin cloth, were common in the Cyclades.

All this evidence, gathered from only one part of the Phourni cemetery, suggests a pronounced Cycladic presence at Archanes during this period. This is only to be expected since research has underlined the intensity of relations between the Cyclades and their nearest neighbour, north-central Crete. Thus it is natural that the flourishing

Prepalatial settlement at Archanes, one of the most important on Crete, should have attracted Cycladic traders. Relations between Crete and the Cyclades manifest themselves clearly in the Minoan cemetery at Phourni where, as we have already seen, some sections are typically Minoan while others such as Tholos Tomb C and the Area of the Rocks betray marked Cycladic features. It will be seen below that these two parts of the cemetery were even more directly associated since it would seem that the deposits absorbed by the Area of the Rocks were, in fact, remains from the clearing of Tholos Tomb C.

One more important discovery from Tholos Tomb C should be mentioned here. This dates from the much later LM IIIA period, almost a thousand years after the burials mentioned above. At this time it seems that funerary offerings were thrown into the tholos tomb from the window next to the tomb's entrance. These are amongst the most characteristic examples of tomb cult at Phourni and included typical examples of the period's pottery such as kylikes and false-spouted amphorae. Fragments of these vases were found above the Prepalatial burial levels in the south-east part of the tholos and underneath the fallen stones of the roof. Their location would indicate that the tholos was still standing intact during the LM IIIA period.

Funerary Building 9

Funerary Building 9 was also used in the MM IA period (ca. 2100-2000 B.C.) Three of its rooms have been excavated, two to the east of Tholos Tomb C and one to the south. The first two rooms contained three successive burial layers in larnakes and pithoi. Some of these burials were surrounded by walls. The third room to the south contained mostly adult burials on the surface, but there were also infant burials in vases and larnakes.

Found in the upper burial layer of the north-west room were two pithoi, one empty and the other containing two burials, and two larnakes, likewise one empty and the other with one burial. Four

95. Two marble Cycladic figurines. From Tholos Tomb C.

96

97

surface burials had been made with limited funerary offerings. The middle burial layer contained three burials in a single larnax and another three surface burials, once again accompanied by only a few offerings. In the third and lowest burial layer, a thin wall closed off the northern part of the room which was used as an ossuary for the deposition of remains from older burials. A few bones and a total of 49 skulls were discovered. The skulls' good condition was due to their having been covered with a fine layer of earth, an act which highlights the special care taken for the dead. The funerary offerings consisted of sea shells and six vases. Four miniature bull figurines were found here as well as two bull rhytons with barbotine and painted decoration, especially interesting examples of the plastic arts during this period. A pithos and a larnax were found empty in the lowest burial layer in the south of this same room, while three skulls were uncovered on the ground. Another notable work of the minor plastic arts came to light in the form of the torso of a terracotta female figurine holding her arms below the breast.

The contents of the north-east room were similar. In the upper burial layer four burials had been made in three larnakes and with limited funerary offerings such as an ivory duck-shaped amulet. In the middle burial layer, one larnax and two pithoi were found with one burial each, while traces of more than one burial were uncovered from the floor together with a few offerings. Finally, the lowest burial layer gave up four larnakes, two of which were empty while the other two had three burials each. Six further burials were found outside the larnakes. A steatite foot- shaped amulet was one of the few funerary offerings found.

The third room in Funerary Building 9 was added onto the south-east side of Tholos Tomb C and contained five ascertained layers with 172 infant and child burials and depositions most of which were made on the surface in small funerary pithoi or pithoid vases, and even in quite a few jars. A child's larnax was also found. Despite the large number of burials and deposits, funerary offerings

96. Five ivory seals from Funerary Building 9. The middle seal is modeled in the shape of a human figure.

97. Ivory amulet in the shape of a crouching monkey. From Funerary Building 9.

could in many instances be identified with the burials they accompanied. In a burial in the first layer, three jars and a fruit-bowl were attributed to a specific burial in the same layer at the northwest corner of the room. The most important offering, however, consisted of a set of five ivory seals which were not only of the same material but also of similar shape, decoration and carving technique, indicating that they may have been the work of the same seal-carver. A unique example amongst these is a plastic seal in the shape of a standing woman clasping her hands below the breast and wearing a long garment with a high bodice and a «collar Medicis» on the shoulder. An ivory pommel from some unknown object was found in a burial from the second layer along with a necklace of seven perforated shells that may have been joined by a biconical meteoric stone bead. In burials from the third layer another two necklaces were found, one with 22 disc-like steatite beads which may have been suspended together with a small bronze bead found together with a juglet; the other had three steatite beads and one of rock crystal.

The second burial layer in the south room of Funerary Building 9 contained one of the excavation's most notable discoveries. This was made adjacent to and west of a pithoid vase containing a child burial and offerings of four vases and a necklace with twelve perforated sea shells. The find in question was a clay model of a seistrum, or rattle, consisting of a wreath-shaped band with two apertures on either side and a hollow handle painted red. Three small perforated clay discs found within the circular band had evidently been attached to wooden rods supported in the middle of the «wreath» by the above mentioned apertures. The regular size of the object and its construction from particularly fine clay does not exclude the possibility that it was actually used as a seistrum.

98. Detail of a figure beating a seistrum, from the famous stone «Harvesters'· Vase» found at Aghia Triada.

99. Clay seistrum found in Funerary Building 9. The three discs were found in situ. The two wooden rods were placed in the original holes during restoration.

98

99

Indeed, it bears marked similarities to one depicted in the procession on the famous Harvesters' Vase from Aghia Triada. The Archanes seistrum may thus constitute the oldest musical instrument in Europe, and it is certainly of exceptional importance for the study of early music in Minoan Crete.

In a more general context, perhaps the most significant finds were the 155 vases of various types found in the south room of Funerary Building 9. These included juglets, two-handled bridge-spouted jars, bowls, fruit-stands, ring-based conical cups (including plain, one-handled and semi-globular varieties), two-handled cups, cooking pots, amphoriskoi, tripod two-handled bridge-spouted jars, and two bell-shaped objects. Finally, other notable finds from the many in this room include gold bands, various steatite and ivory amulets (such as a fine crouching monkey), and many seals. All these funerary offerings go to suggest the wealth of those buried in this room.

Funerary Building 13

Of Funerary Building 13 (whose remains lie under those of Funerary Building 9) only a few wall foundations survive on the rock surface. The little information gleaned by the excavations points to a funerary building with MM IA burials (before 2100 B.C.) made on a layer of stones similar to that encountered in Tholos Tomb C. Uncovered together with the remnants of a possible child's burial were a gold bird-shaped cut-out decorated in the repousee technique, part of a blade, an obsidian chip and eight sea shells.

FUNERARY BUILDINGS 18 AND 19

A narrow passageway immediately south of Tholos Tomb C and the south room of Funerary Building 9 separated these buildings from three others immediately to the south. These were the large Funerary Building 18 which rested on the scanty remains of the older Funerary Building 24, and further to the south-west the apsidal Funerary Building 19. Funerary Buildings 18 and 19 are of especial importance in that they represent the only buildings in the cemetery at Phourni with MM burials (after 2000 B.C.)

Funerary Building 18

Funerary Building 18 is one of the largest such buildings at Phourni with a total of ten rooms. The three south rooms without an approach were without doubt the first built (during the MM IA period, ca. 2100-2000 B.C.) and included burial deposits, sometimes in layers, of the type found in many other of the cemetery's funerary buildings, and accompanied by the usual funerary offerings of pottery, seals, amulets and necklaces made of sea shells.

The seven northern-most rooms with MM II burials (ca. 1800 B.C.) were built later. The northern labyrinthine rooms, approached from the east, were exceptionally well constructed with paved floors in some, and others rooved with large slab-like stones water-proofed with soft stone chippings. These rooms were mostly used for individual burials in larnakes and pithoi, as well as surface burials. Of these, the two west rooms were particularly crowded. All in all, the north rooms contained 48 burials of which 14 were made in larnakes and nine in an equivalent number of pithoi; the remaining 15 were surface burials. One larnax contained a couple of bodies whose skeletons were perfectly preserved.

The north-west room alone contained 16 burials in four successive layers. In the upper burial layer a small larnax and two child surface burials were discovered with an unusual vase as an offering. The second layer contained a tub larnax along the south wall, and another chest larnax along the north. A pithos stood immediately to the right of the doorway. One burial each had taken place in the larnakes while two had been interred in the pithos. The same layer provided two surface burials. Only one larnax existed in the third layer, along the length of the west wall with an offering of a stepped pyramidal ivory seal. Yet another surface burial was encountered here. Finally, in the fourth layer, one larnax each was placed along the north, south, and west walls; a pithos stood to the left of the doorway with two surface burials, one accompanied by an ivory seal.

The many funerary offerings which accompanied the other burials in the north rooms were equally important not only for their seals of ivory and precious stones but also for their pottery and stone vases. A few burials in the eastern rooms of Funerary Building 18 were accompanied by significant Kamares ware vases: jugs, cups, bridge-spouted jugs, a tubular vessel and three stone vases of which one was a kernos. The shapes and decoration of the larnakes and burial pithoi are also of great interest. The outer base of one larnax pre-

100. Twin stone vase from Funerary Building 19.

serves the imprint of a straw mat while one of the pithoi is unique with its incised and plastic medallion decoration. The exceptional state of preservation of the skeletal material from the north rooms, moreover, made it necessary for especial care to be taken during excavation so as to preserve not only an accurate picture of the architectural remains, but also serve the interests of anthropological research.

Clearly, the north section of Funerary Building 18 is one of the most important in the cemetery at Phourni. Quite apart from its construction and the preservation of the skeletal remains, the discovery of individualised MM burials sheds new light on burial customs during this period.

Funerary Building 19

Funerary Building 19, the only apsidal funerary structure in Crete, was used for burials and depositions during the MM IA and the beginning of the MM IB period (namely, from approximately 2100 to 1950 B.C.)

This apsidal building is roughly inscribed within a square with an entrance to the south-west. The double-walls surrounding the three sides of the apse are unusually thick, evidently for the support of the building with its vaulted roof. This is clearly apparent from the east side where the wall surface recedes slightly, as well as from the fallen stones of the roof found therein.

The excavation discerned two burial layers, one upper and another lower, without a clear chronological differentiation between them. Burials in vases and larnakes (mostly childrens') predominated in the upper layer. The lower layer was mostly taken up with adult surface burials while in comparison with the upper layer the amount of vases decreased dramatically. Thus in the upper burial layer of Funerary Building 19, 76 burials were identified of which many certainly belonged to children. While a total of five child larnakes were found, child burials in vases was generally the rule. These vases were mostly large and medium sized jars, but pithoid vases were also found together with tripod pyxides with lids, and tripod cooking pots. More than one burial was found in some of the larger vessels. Apart from the skull (or the skull and the bones) found inside the burial vases, funerary offerings also existed along with smaller vases and various small objects,

101

101. Clay animal figurines and rhytons from various locations in the Phourni Cemetery.

102. Selection of pottery from Funerary Building 19.

103. Clay bridge - spouted vase with plastic and painted decoration. From Funerary Building 19.

102

mostly beads from necklaces, but including animal or bird bones and sea shells. Surface burials, including those of children, were also evident.

As we saw above, the amount of offerings – pottery in particular – accompanying the burials was large. A total of 137 vases were found from the upper burial layer of Funerary Building 19, including many and varied shapes often intriguingly decorated. This number, furthermore, does not include the larger burial vases already indicated. A unique pithoid vase was adorned with plastic branches and painted drop pendants. Of the other finds from the upper layer, mention can be made of three stone vases, two silver rings, eight various bronze objects, twelve obsidian blades and 25 beads of various materials. A child burial gave up a terracotta female figurine depicted in a long garment.

The burials in the lower layer of Funerary Building 19 were very compressed with the result that a particular attribution of specific offerings to any of the 105 burials identified was difficult. Unlike the upper layer, only two of these burials were identified as being of children, while the fact that all the lower burials were made on the surface constitutes a distinguishing feature between both layers. Vases were typically less in the lower layer, totaling 45 although containing a variety of shapes including a kalathos and a small pithoid jar. On the other hand, the lower burial layer was richer in precious objects such as figurines, amulets and seals.

Of the two terracotta figurines found, the most important renders a tetrapod of some description with disc-like perforated protuberances instead of legs. Five amulets and three of the four seals were made of ivory. One of these is a cylinder seal with a square attachment for suspension at the top. Of exceptional workmanship, it is decorated with leaf motifs in two successive rows between spirals executed with light incisions over the entire surface of the cylinder. Other finds include a gold band, 26 obsidian blades, 16 necklace beads of ivory, bone, rock crystal, faience and steatite, over 100 sea shells, and animal and bird bones.

THOLOS TOMB E AND FUNERARY BUILDING 16

Tholos Tomb E and Funerary Building 16 abutting on its south side are the southern-most funerary complexes in the cemetery at Phourni and the closest to the Minoan settlement. Although Tholos Tomb D is more to the south, it seems to have been an isolated structure rather than an integral part of the cemetery complex.

Tholos Tomb E

Tholos Tomb E is perhaps the first funerary building to have been built at Phourni seeing that its lower burial layer is dated to EM II (ca. 2400-2300 B.C.) As with the slightly later Tholos Tomb C, Tholos Tomb E was also built above ground; although it is not as well preserved due to the downward incline of the hill and subsequent cultivation of the area. The doorway in the eastern side was flanked by two monolithic antae and it is possible that a large flat stone a few metres to the east, and now overturned, was employed as the lintel.

Tholos Tomb E was undisturbed and contained two burial layers with a intervening chronological gap of two hundred years, the latter layer being dated to MM IA (between 2100-2000 B.C.) In the lower EM II layer, many burials must have taken place, as the number of funerary offerings seems to indicate. No less than 117 offerings were found made of ivory, marble, gypsum, obsidian, quartz, schist, steatite, bone, clay, and even bronze and gold. The burials, however, were leveled during the formation of the upper burial layer, thus making it impossible to identify them during the excavations. It is certain, on the other hand, that the burials had been made on the surface and in at least two larnakes – whose lids were found.

Noteworthy amongst the funerary offerings of the lower burial layer are eight seals of steatite, schist and ivory with linear motifs on the sealing surface; some of the earliest firmly dated seals of this type from Minoan Crete. Significant amongst them is an ivory theriomorphic seal with two plastic animal busts, possibly snakes, inter-coiling from opposite directions, and a cross-hatch motif on the sealing surface. A small globular vase with four apertures for suspension at the lip and a lid decorated with thick incised lines is an important find for this date since a parallel exists from Koumasa. Perhaps the most notable offering after the 26 ivory amulets is a Cycladic figurine found together with an alabastron, a marble vase and a steatite amulet.

Tholos Tomb E, as we saw, was reused for burials in the MM IA period after having been unutilised for some two hundred years. The upper burial layer from this period was better preserved, containing a total of 56 burials, 36 of which were made in 29 larnakes and two pithoi while the others constituted surface burials between the larnakes. The larnakes themselves had been placed one progressively closer to the other going from north-west to south-east. Some were chest and others tub larnakes; three tiny larnakes may have been used for child burials. The first larnakes in the tomb were placed close to the tholos wall and then gradated to the centre, thus leaving the space in front of the entrance free. The last larnax was placed between the antae of the doorway. Due to the crowded nature of the area, it was necessary to place one on top of the other thus creating three tiers of larnakes, the remains of which, however, belong to the upper burial layer. Many larnakes were preserved only in fragments without any burials being discernible although it seems that only one burial was made in each. However, some isolated examples exist of two, three, four, or even seven burials in one larnax. The fact that some larnakes bore painted script is of exceptional interest.

Once again, of amongst the total of 137 offerings uncovered here and made of ivory, bone, clay, faience, bronze, silver, alabaster, amethyst, gypsum, marble, meteorite, rock crystal, and sard, it is the seals which take pride of place. More specifically, twelve conical, disc, button, three-sided, and cylindrical seals were found of faience, steatite, meteorite, rock crystal and ivory. Most of these had linear motifs on the sealing surface or so-called architectural motifs, as well as animal representations; one seal with a depiction of lions is one such an example. Especially interesting for its shape is a bronze signet ring with linear motifs. Other finds from Tholos Tomb E include three necklaces reassembled from scattered beads, a terracotta bell-shaped figurine, animal bones, and twelve sea shells.

Funerary Building 16

Funerary Building 16 abuts Tholos Tomb E to the south and is not well preserved, particularly to the south and east, due once again to the downward incline of the surface and subsequent cultivation. It comprises two wings to the east and west with one and two rooms respectively. These wings are not divided by a partition but have separate walls sharing a common passage running

104

104. Necklace made of amethyst and sard. From Tholos Tomb E.

between them. Funerary Building 16 was used for burials during the MM IA period (*ca.* 2100-2000 B.C.)

The burial layer in the single room of the west wing had been disturbed. It is certain, however, that it contained burials in at least one chest larnax since fragments of at least three skulls were found together with various funerary offerings. The burials in the east wing were better preserved. The burial layer in the north room of the wing consisted of six chest larnakes containing a total of eleven burials, with one to five burials in each larnax. Seven surface burials were also found. The offerings included two vases, a bronze cutter, animal bones and four seals one of which was made of faience in the shape of a seated beast. An interesting find was a bronze earring found *in situ* on a skull in the north-west corner.

Four pithoi and two larnakes (one a chest and the other a tub larnax) were found in the south room of the east wing of Funerary Building 16. A skull was found in one larnax, three in the other, one each in two of the pithoi, and 17 more on the floor between the larnakes. The funerary offerings, all of which were found outside both the

105. Clay pyxis from Tholos Tomb D. The necklace in fig. 111 was found within.

larnakes and the pithoi, included five clay vases, three ivory amulets and three steatite and ivory seals. One of the ivory seals, shaped like a flattened cylinder, bore a foliate motif on one sealing-surface and on the other a depiction of a man carrying two vases on a plank of wood supported on his shoulder.

Tholos Tomb D

The southern-most building at Phourni is Tholos Tomb D, the excavation of which revealed an undisturbed and rich female burial dated to LM IIIA2 (*ca.* 1350-1300 B.C.), slightly after the undisturbed royal burial of Tholos Tomb A.

Tholos Tomb D is hewn from hard rock, part of which was employed as a section of the tholos wall. The rest of this wall was constructed from small and large stones in irregular horizontal ring-shaped courses. The tomb is significantly smaller than that of Tholos Tomb A and its state of preservation modest due to the collapse of the roof.

Entrance was made from the south; and the tomb floor inclines north-west to south-east. Perhaps this irregularity was rectified by the laying of earth brought from outside, in which case the existence of larnax fragments found in the lower layer during excavations would be explained. If not, they must belong to some earlier burial.

That only one female burial took place in Tholos Tomb D was clearly indicated by the funerary offerings. The body had been placed with its head against the south-east wall of the tholos and its feet facing south-west resting on a wooden support. Despite the disturbance to the burial occasioned by the collapse of the roof, the skeleton's position and even the use of the various offerings and the position of jewelery worn by the deceased were determined with certainty. The dead woman held a bronze mirror with her left hand just in front of her face. On her head she wore a single gold diadem of 37 rectangular beads depicting double argonaut motifs, while three necklaces adorned her breast. The first of these consisted of 50 beads: 20 granular and globular beads made of gold, 29 of glass paste and one of sard. The second was made up of 32 faience beads and the third of 15 drop-like beads, also of faience. 13 drop-shaped beads of electrum found in a very fragmentary form should perhaps be attributed to the third necklace: it is noteworthy that this material is very rare in Minoan Crete. Another eight glass-paste papyrus-shaped beads must have belonged to the second or third necklace.

The adornment undertaken on the dead woman did not, of course, neglect her hair (two locks of which would undoubtedly have been gathered by two gold rings found *in situ*), or her gown held at the shoulder by two glass-paste pins, or the gold-trimmed material that covered her head and shoulders. 67 gold beads with twelve-petal rosettes on one side should be attributed to the latter garment. That these beads originated from a piece of fabric – and not from a necklace – is confirmed not only by the fact that only one visible side was decorated, but also by the holes at the edges from

106. Reconstruction of the burial in Tholos Tomb D with the utensils and jewelery as they were found.

107. Detail of the burial in Tholos Tomb D during the excavations.

107

108. Gold beads originally woven on the peplos of the dead woman in Tholos Tomb D.

109. Pin made of glass paste and necklaces with gold, faience, glass paste and sard beads. From Tholos Tomb D.

109

110. Gold diadem from the burial in Tholos Tomb D.

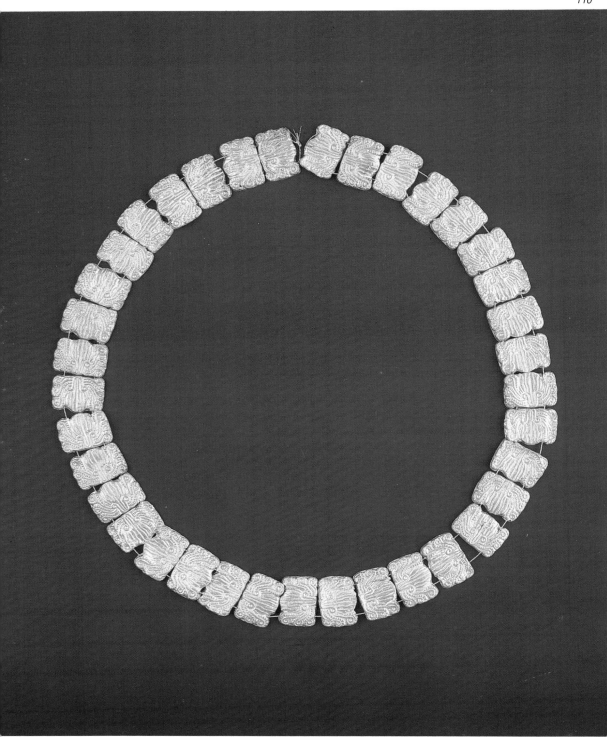

111. Necklace from the burial in Tholos Tomb D. Found within the pyxis shown in fig. 105.

112. Clay anthropomorphic rhyton found in the Area of the Rocks.

which they could be sewn on. A similar gold bead which did belong to the necklace in the pyxis has only one hole, this time clearly for suspension and decorated on both sides. Finally, a small silver ring was found near the skeleton together with a smaller lentoid jasper seal-stone – perhaps the smallest Minoan seal-stone ever found – and a few pieces of ivory too fragmented to determine its original form.

The deceased's wealth in life, however, was greater than that she wore to the grave. For, just as with the undisturbed royal burial of Tholos Tomb A, other items of jewelery were made as offerings apart from those which adorned the body. Placed to the north of the woman's head was a large, heavily ornamented clay pyxis with a lid wherein were found a bronze razor-like triangular knife, a few ivory fragments which may have belonged to the handle of the knife, and a singular necklace together with a rock-crystal amulet in the shape of a figure-of-eight shield. Apart from one glass paste bead and another of faience, the necklace contained in the pyxis consisted of gold beads which were not, however, of uniform shape (as is common) but of various types from the perspective of both motif and technique: indeed, here we have a veritable repertoire of beads from this period. With this lavish addition of yet another significant necklace to the burial, the wealth of

the woman interred in Tholos Tomb D at Archanes is clearly attested. This is no doubt the most important burial at Phourni after Tholos Tomb A, and must be considered that of a person of royal blood.

The roof of Tholos Tomb D seems to have collapsed at the end of the Mycenaean period in Crete. On top of its roughly levelled ruins three burials were found with offerings of bronze rings (one of which was found on a hand of one of the dead) and a bronze fibula dated to the Sub-Minoan period. This find indicates that the cemetery at Phourni continued in use up till the end of the 11th century B.C., namely for 1,400 years.

THE AREA OF THE ROCKS

As has been stated frequently, the unique organization of the Phourni cemetery hardly left any space to be unutilised. Many tens of burials from various periods, frequently with important funerary offerings, were found in almost all the areas between the buildings described above. It would be impossible here to mention all of these. However, in order that some understanding of the cemetery's organization be arrived at, it is essential that a brief mention be made of excavations conducted over a large area in the south-west section of the cemetery to the west and along the length (from north to south) of Funerary Buildings 6, 23, and 5, Tholos Tomb C, and Funerary Buildings 22, 18, and 19. This elongated area is full of large slab-like rocks on the surface separated by narrow fissures. The entire area here was used in Prepalatial times and although this use was not uniform, as the excavations showed, it was ancillary to that of the neighbouring buildings.

In the north part of the Area of the Rocks, west of Funerary Buildings 6, 12, and 5 and around Funerary Building 23, depositions of burial remains took place (most probably from the neighbouring Funerary Buildings) accompanied by funerary offerings. In the central area to the north, west of Tholos Tomb C, burials also took place. A large number of vases came to light here together with many other finds, mostly figurines, and including a unique terracotta anthropomorphic rhyton and three important Cycladic figurines. In the central area to the south, south-west of Funerary Building 22, pottery fragments and bones were absorbed into the surface together with a few funerary offerings.

Finally, in the south part of the Area of the Rocks, west of Funerary Buildings 18 and 19, depositions of burial remains were made, possibly from Tholos Tomb C. Over a thousand obsidian blades were found here together with scattered bones and other objects similar to those found in Tholos Tomb C; a bronze pin and a lead cut-out, for example. A gold cylindrically shaped bead with incisions, uncovered here, is of the same type as others found in Tholos Tomb C which belonged to two necklaces. The most important evidence, however, of an interconnection between both these areas is constituted by the eight marble Cycladic figurines and (just as in Tholos Tomb C) fragments of idols – heads and feet – belonging to separate figurines. Of interest here are two heads (one 0.08m. high) belonging to a large figurine, and a male torso fragment.

THE QUARRY

West-north-west of the Area of the Rocks, to the west of the cemetery and, more specifically, at a distance some 46m. from Tholos Tomb C, and at the summit of the hill looking down onto the town, Iouktas, and the road to Anemospilia, are traces of part of the cemetery's quarry. This is a rectangular area of notable dimensions (2.60 x 2.45m.) sunk into the flat limestone from which slabs were quarried. Certain traces of tool-marks can be seen, perhaps made by a crowbar, as well as the grooves which facilitated the splitting of the rock. The blocks quarried here were undoubtedly used in the construction of the cemetery buildings and possibly of Tholos Tomb B.

The quarry at Phourni is not, of course, the only Minoan quarry in Crete. The most well known of these, however, exist in close proximity to palaces or settlements. It is thus significant that the Phourni quarry is the only Minoan quarry to serve a cemetery. This clearly was an added reason as to why Phourni was chosen as the specific location for the cemetery whose 26 Funerary Buildings described above were constructed from the rock quarried here.

THE SHRINES

Archanes lies in the shadow of Mt. Iouktas, the most important mountain in the wider vicinity of Knossos. The sheer height of this mountain must have played an important role in early seafaring as it constitutes the first landmark on the horizon for anyone sailing to Knossos. From the north-west, Iouktas resembles the giant outline of a reclining male head.

Iouktas may be considered the sacred mountain of Archanes since the devotional activities of the vicinity have been concentrated there from Antiquity right up till today. Four ancient shrines are located thereon: two on the sites Psili Korfi and Anemospilia and another two in the caves Hosto Nero and Stravomyti. Even today, the most important centre of worship for the people of Archanes is the church of Christ the Lord (*Affendis Christos*) on the mountain.

Psili Korfi

The shrine of Psili Korfi on the mountains' highest point was discovered and excavated for the first time by Evans. This is the most important peak sanctuary in Crete, a fact borne out all and more by the excavations currently conducted there by the Greek Archaeological Society. The shrine, which comprises a temenos (or sacred precinct), is made up of an open area on three levels with rooms that may have served as cult areas or dwellings for the priests. There is also a crevice whose sacred character is betrayed by the bronze double-axes found therein.

A great number of votive offerings were found here, in particular terracotta anthropomorphic and zoomorphic figurines and stone offering tables, as well as personal items such as seals and beads. Since many of these objects were associated with finds from the palace centre, the settlement, and the Phourni cemetery, Evans may well have been correct in hypothesising that a road once led from the eastern-most part of the settlement (Troullos) to the peak sanctuary. Furthermore, he himself had established that traces existed of just such a paved Minoan road at Anemospilia and Psili Korfi.

Cult practices at Psili Korfi followed the fortunes of the palace centre and the settlement of Archanes. The worship of Poseidon, refereed to in the inscription from Argos mentioned above, undoubtedly had some relation to the prehistoric worship of the young god at this very place.

The Cave of Hosto Nero

Travellers of the last century were already familiar with this cave, situated at a height of 720m. on the west slope of Iouktas.

An antechamber leads on to three entrances, the two narrow- most leading to low apartments via arcade-like passages formed by the natural rock. Access to the lower of these is difficult. The passage to the right is 10m. long and leads on the right to a room some 10 x 2m. with four pillars. The passage to the left branches out into two upper passages which are not easily accessible, with the possible exception of the central one. All are covered with stalactites while the one to the right also contains water.

The finds here were not too plentiful. Cult use began in the MM period and continued up to the Greek period with only one interruption according the finds recovered till now.

The Stravomyti Cave

The cave is located on the south-west slope of Iouktas at a height of 400m., and was also mentioned by travellers during the last century. The older excavations uncovered remains here extending from Neolithic up to Greek.

The cave consists of a network of raised natural passageways with five entrances, two large areas above and one below, and with an enclosed pond and stalactites. The passageways are 5m. wide, the longest being 40m.

In Neolithic times, the cave was used for burial or as a place of refuge, and certainly as a dwelling area in the EM period, as evinced by the exceptional pottery of that period found therein. From the MM period onwards, the cave may have been used as a

113. View of part of Iouktas with the Stravomyti Cave, from the west.

storage place for cereals but was undoubtedly also a venue for worship, and continued as such into the LM and Geometric periods. The baetyl found near the entrance comes from the latter period. The Stravomyti cave was once considered the shrine of some female deity such as Eileithyia, Dictyna or Artemis, and even of aqueous or chthonic deities.

Anemospilia

One of the most important sites in the vicinity of Archanes is Anemospilia (Caves of the Wind). It was here, an area so appropriately named by the locals due to its many and wind-swept caves, that the earliest temple in Crete not associated with any other structure or settlement was discovered in 1979. Furthermore, a macabre and unique discovery was made therein: the remains of a human sacrifice. This shrine, one of the most important in Minoan Crete, was located and excavated by J. and E. Sakellarakis in 1979 during an investigation of the north slope of Iouktas in the course of a field survey of the Archanes area.

Anemospilia is located some 400m. lower than Psili Korfi at the vantage point where the ancient roads meet, and is blessed with a breathtaking view. From here one can see Mt. Dikti to the east, Mt. Ida to the west, as well as all the large and small centres of the north coast: Knossos, Herakleion, and the Aegean Sea stretching out towards Greece.

On a small tongue of land jutting out precisely at the point where the rocky mountain bed and cultivatable land start to converge, an important structure was built of which four areas have till now been excavated, although other ancillary quarters may exist. The thick walls of this sturdy building were covered with white or red plaster decorated with bands, which at some points has survived. The use of ashlar poros-stone masonry was lavish in the thresholds and antae, which at some points bore masons' marks such as a cross.

What impresses one here, however, is not so much the refinement of construction as much as

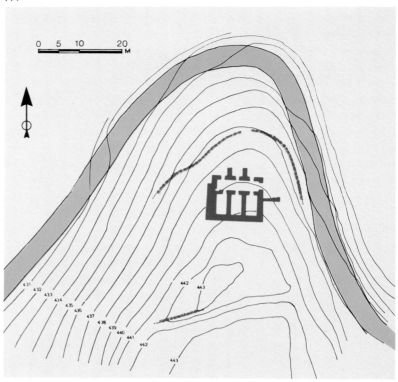

114

114. Ground plan of the
Anemospilia shrine.

115. View of the shrine at
Anemospilia from the south.

the plan and the structures' integration into the area. Here we have a rectangular building with three closed rooms of equal size to the south, and a long corridor to the north as wide as the three rooms together. The simple symmetry of the ground plan is unusual in Minoan architecture which is normally characterised by complex, labyrinthine structures. The northern orientation of the building (with a slight deviation) is shared by the Minoan palaces. An enclosure wall discovered to the north and south is likewise characteristic and undoubtedly surrounded the building and the sacred precinct on all sides.

To the time of writing, this building at Anemospilia has no parallel in the Cretan-Mycenaean world, even though its architectural features are known from art works depicting tripartite shrines, for instance the gold cut-outs from Mycenae and Volos, the stone rhyton from Zakros, and the Archanes ring. Moreover, recent studies have determined that these works portray independent shrines on mountain slopes, the typology of which was later transferred to domestic complexes such that at Vathypetro and the palace at Knossos.

This exceptional structure at Anemospilia clearly had all the characteristics of both a temenos and a shrine, similar to those which crystallised in the later

Greek period, or even those contemporary to Minoan Crete in Cyprus, the East and Egypt (the temple of Phta at Karnak, to take one example). Also important is the fact that the Anemospilia shrine bears clear features that not only enable a reconstruction of a tripartite shrine but also throw light on the predetermined devotional ritual employed therein.

The central room is differentiated from the antechamber by a threshold slightly higher than that of the other rooms, while the special position of the west room is accentuated by an alcove, adjacent to a stairway, which may have been decorated with frescoes. The many utensils and other evidence found during the excavations impress one with the strict adherence paid to structural arrangements associated with the requirements of ceremonial ritual. The efforts made to arrange the shrines' architectural plan were, moreover, clearly reflected in the organisation of its various utensils and trappings.

The antechamber would no doubt have been the venue for the preparation of ritual acts. This is strongly suggested by the find of some 150 vases of various shapes, including a noteworthy cup of communion, as well as pithoi, pestles and tripod

115

cooking pots. The pithoi, some of which had been incised with signs of script, were normally used in shrines to store woven materials as well as liquid and solid foodstuffs essential for ritual ceremonies. The cooking pots and pestles were no doubt used for the preparation of these provisions.

We know from contemporary civilizations in the East and Egypt that offerings to the gods were not always homogeneous, but that an admixture was often made. This appears to explain the presence of the many mortars and pestles found in the antechamber. The *popana*, *pemmata* (a sweet bread), and the *plakountes* were a few of the edible preparations offered to the deity and recorded by Athenaeus along with other fanciful Cretan recipes. Some of these were offered baked, others unbaked; some with bones and others without, as Euaenetus informs us in his *Opsartytikon* where he mentions a certain *myma*, or admixture of small pieces of boneless meat. Thus it comes as no surprise that bones were not found in the antechamber and, indeed, even in those areas where cooking pots were uncovered, with the exception of a point in the west section where they were associated with clay trays.

Bench-like structures in the antechamber served not only as seats but also as a repository for utensils. A stone structure at the entrance of the central room was most likely used for libations in front of the double wooden door whose existence is betrayed by traces of hinges in the poros-stone threshold.

The central room was packed with the shrines' larger vessels and utensils. Apart from pithoi found along the length of the walls, the entire floor was covered with vases, with the exception of the south and south-west section. The latter area was taken up by a bench some 0.25m. high carved from the natural rock and running along the south wall. At the corner, however, where the bench rose to some 0.40m. above the floor, the rock surface remained in its natural state. A rhyton and a bucket had been placed on the bench, which had been covered with yellow earth brought from outside; these were objects with a specific ritual use. Furthermore, it was here that a find of exceptional interest came to light: a pair of out-size clay feet with the upper surface finely finished and terminating in a dowel. It seems clear that this find was originally located on the bench, whence it fell. More intriguingly, a thick layer of ash from some wooden object was discovered around it, thus providing a clue as to its eventual interpretation.

Similar models of feet have been found in various parts of Crete: at Gournia, Malia, Sklavokambos, as well as on Kea. They have been variously interpreted as everything from shoe-anvils to votive offerings. All the locations in which they have been found, however, included cult objects, but not a single votive offering. Thus the interpretations given above must be reconsidered. As far as the Archanes feet are concerned, however, they preserve significant details which suggest their use, namely the dowels on the upper surfaces used for the insertion and support of a wooden body. A comparison of these feet with those under the clay skirts of terracotta figurines of female deities from the Sub-Minoan shrine at Karfi is instructive. Just as with these figurines, so the Archanes feet must have been obscured by some garment covering the wooden body. The contextual discovery of ash and pieces of burnt wood with the Archanes feet permits their interpretation as the remains of a large wooden acrolithic idol, namely a statue whose extremities were made of materials other than that of the main body.

The acrolithic technique is known in the Aegean from Neolithic times, and in Crete from the MM period in particular. Indeed, large clay heads have been discovered at the peak sanctuaries of Petsofas, Psili Korfi on Iouktas, and Kofinas. Found in the palace at Knossos were a stone wig, a braid (similar to that found at Mycenae), and bronze locks of hair. From the palace at Phaistos we have a mould for the casting of a bronze human hand which underscores the variety of materials used for the construction of the extremities. Finally, a small stone wig has been associated with the ivory body of a figurine from Palaikastro. It seems, then, that there were large cult statues in Minoan Crete of the xoanon, or wooden idol, type. It is no coincidence that Pausanias linked the word xoanon with the epithet «ancient», and associated it with the Cretan Daedalus. A similar idol is no doubt depicted on the Kamares fruit-bowl from Phaistos and on a clay sealing from Aghia Triada where two figures are depicted attiring the idol.

The offering of raiments to the cult idol, together with its ritual investiture, are known both from Aegean iconography (such as the Thera frescoes) and from the Greek period where the xoanon, attired with real garments, is depicted on coins and vases and mentioned by ancient writers. Furthermore, we also know of the rituals involved in the idols cleansing and beautifying (*plentyria* and *kallynteria* in Attica, and the feast of the Tonaia of Samos). The xoana most often mentioned are those of Hera, Demetra, Eileithyia, Dionysos and Apollo. All these deities have a pre-hellenic origin, such as Britomartis and Artemis whose Minoan origins are attested. Remains of Greek and Roman acrolithic statues have been found in many areas and a certain amount of information even exists on the type of wood used in their construction as well as of the fabric used for the vestments. We know from Minoan depictions of idol investiture that the garment was often fringed and embroidered with zig-zag or scale patterns commonly worn by priests. Thus in most aspects, the graphic reconstruction of the Archanes xoanon may be considered accurate.

The xoanon would have dominated the central room of the Anemospilia shrine, standing next to the natural rock left bare on purpose to represent the «sacred earth». In just the same manner, Kallikrates left a section of the rock of the Athenian Acropolis bare in a niche below the temple of Athena Nike. The vases found left and right were remnants of offerings made to the cult idol after both ritual bloodless and blood sacrifices were made in separate areas. Typical of the finds here was a jug containing carbonized fruit. Perhaps the final offerings were made directly onto the natural rock.

The eastern room was undoubtedly the venue for bloodless ritual ceremonies. This spacious chamber included a man-made stepped altar against the south wall. Four pithoi stood by the east wall; other utensils were placed on shelves (whose existence was verified by the excavations) while another group was left on the floor. Most of the objects in this area were small, including many clay vases and two tiny bronze boxes with apertures, perhaps for a thread. One of these boxes had a small tube in place of the hole, possibly a hermetic seal for the contents. These boxes are very similar to a gold specimen found in Grave Circle A at Mycenae, and also to two more gold examples found in the Mycenaean royal burial of Tholos Tomb A in the Phourni cemetery at Archanes. They may have contained some significant substance and were thus used as charms.

The structure at the back of the room was grounded in the natural rock. This was a stepped altar of a well-known type certified by actual examples such as that in the central court of the palace

116. Clay cup of communion from the corridor of the Anemospilia shrine.

117. View from the north of the central room of the Anemospilia shrine during the excavations.

118. Clay feet, larger than natural size, from the central room of the Anemospilia shrine. The square dowel at the top was used to attach the wooden body of the xoanon.

117

118

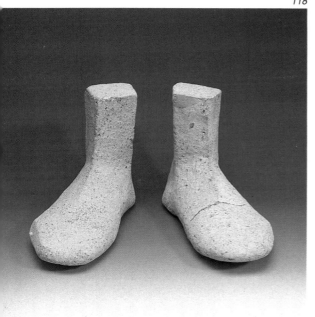

at Phaistos and in the palace and Theatre Area at Archanes, but also by depictions such as that on the Zakros rhyton and the larnax from Aghia Triada, where it is found next to a tree and in front of a figure at a smaller-scale which has, indeed, been interpreted as a xoanon. On the Zakros rhyton, a branch is depicted on the altar: the symbol of a bloodless sacrifice.

Ritual vessels and utensils were found on top of the stepped altar in the east room. Of the large basin-like dishes, one had been positioned in the centre and bore a carved Linear-A inscription on the rim. This vessel finds an exact parallel in that depicted in a relief vase fragment from Knossos where precisely the same scene is depicted: a mountain shrine area with a venerant devoutly bending down to offer his dish. That these deep dishes were intended for offerings of fruits of the earth is known from the Aghia Triada larnax where the same object is accompanied by other vessels meant for liquid and bloodless offerings, such as a libation jug. It come then as little surprise to find that just such a jug was found here in the east room itself. Liquid offerings must have been many at Anemospilia judging by the host of jug types whose varied shapes and decoration may have acted as an indication of the specific substance contained therein.

Other items which accompanied ritual acts in the east room included a portable stone altar with a depression in the centre of its upper surface, and three small and exceptionally handsome kalyx-like goblets one of which was adorned with an insert depicting some kind of flower. Similar goblets are known from other parts of Archanes and, interestingly, other examples, this time of faience, are known from the Temple Repository at Knossos and the earlier Grave Circle B at Mycenae. Also found in the east room was an askos painted with floral motifs in a burnished yellow colour. It has been suggested that these askoi were decorated with paintings of the analogous plant used in the preparation stored therein.

Together with fruit, crops and vegetables, liquids such as wine and oil, and, perhaps, the aromatic herbs contained in the vases of the east room, another natural element was found whose presence

119. Reconstruction of the central room of the Anemospilia shrine with the utensils and the vases as found, and the xoanon as it would have appeared supported on the clay feet.

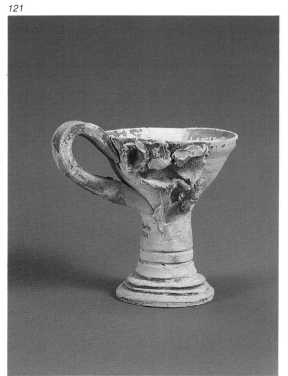

121

120. Selection of pottery from the east room of the Anemospilia shrine. A few of these vases were found on the stepped altar shown in fig. 123.

121, 122. Small ornate clay cup with plastic flower attachment, and a steatite table of offerings. Found respectively on the left part of the upper step and on the lower step of the altar in fig. 123.

122

123. Reconstruction of the stepped altar on the south wall of the east room of the Anemospilia shrine. The vases and utensils are shown in the location in which they were found.

124. View of the north part of the east room of the Anemospilia shrine with the three fallen pithoi as found during the excavations.

123

124

is significant: pebbles from the sea shore. We know from the sea shells found in the Temple Repository at Knossos and in other shrines that the marine world constituted an indelible element of worship. Here, then, in the eastern room at Anemospilia where bloodless sacrifices were offered, the vegetal world and the sea prevail.

Prior to discussing the west room where other ritual acts took place, a short word must be said concerning the date and nature of the catastrophe which destroyed the shrine at Anemospilia, and after which it was never reused.

The excavations indicated that only an earthquake could possibly have caused the catastrophe, throwing down the walls with their huge finely-hewn blocks. This is quite clear from the manner and the incline in which the blocks and the large pithoi fell. All the objects found appeared to have fallen and, furthermore, no trace of violent enemy invasion was discerned, nor would it be expected given that it is widely accepted that the *Pax Minoica* prevailed in Crete at this time. The ensuing fire, caused by the lamps (uncovered during the excavations) which lit the otherwise dark shrine, helped complete the work of destruction wrought by the terrible earthquake. It was this fire which consumed the wooden parts of the xoanon together with the buildings' shelves and wooden fittings.

The date of this catastrophe must be placed in the first half of the 17th century B.C., at a time when the MM II and IIIA pottery styles flourished. Examples of precisely this style, including fine polychrome Kamares ware, were found in the shrine itself. The ascertainment of this date helps bridge the many chronological gaps between the poorly stratified older excavations at Knossos and the latest ones at Phaistos. The implications of the Anemospilia shrines' chronology are important since here we have a structure that effectively constitutes a «closed» find with a short and defined lifespan of a few decades covering its construction, operation, and final destruction.

The earthquake destruction is also confirmed by a significant discovery made between the doorway of the central room and that of the antechamber: more specifically, the skeletal remains of a human being under a pile of fallen blocks. The skeletons' condition did not permit conclusions as to sex or age. On the other hand, it is certain that the person was crushed by stones crashing down from above after having fallen on his stomach while attempting to leave the central room. His pose was reconstructed with the help of signs of damage to the back part of one of the relatively well- preserved tibia. The discovery of a human skeleton inside a Minoan shrine is as extraordinary as it is important, especially when one considers that in almost a century of excavations human finds have very rarely been discovered in locations other than cemeteries. For this reason, it has often been maintained that at the first signs of the first pre-seismic tremors people took their most valuable possessions and left their houses promptly.

Also significant is the fact that an extremely rare Kamares relief vase was found in fragments at the feet of the skeleton and in the entrance to the central room. This is one of the most important vases to have come to light in Crete, and was probably being held by the deceased as he left the central room, a scene which the reader can see reconstructed in the fine illustrations made to the authors' specifications by N. Giannadakis and included in this volume. This unique vase is of the same shape as the buckets found in front of the xoanon in the east room and, more importantly, this is precisely the same type of vase as that depicted on the Aghia Triada larnax depicting a bull-sacrifice, where it lies under the altar to collect the blood of the slaughtered beast. Moreover, on the Archanes vase a white bull is shown in relief reminiscent of depictions of the Egyptian god Apis, and between branches and relief rosettes, all rendered in the fine polychrome Kamares technique in white, black, and red with applied incisions. Crocuses and spirals complete the decoration which finds its only iconographic parallel in a vase from Phaistos where two goats (likewise a sacrificial animal) are depicted with rosettes.

Together with the bovine and goat bones found in the western part of the antechamber in trays similar to those held by priests in the frescoes from the palace at Pylos, the bull vase constitutes clear proof that, just as the east room had been the venue for bloodless sacrifices, so the west chamber was reserved for sacrifices of blood.

From the outset, this room had presented the excavators with a puzzling asymmetry in its architec-

125. Reconstruction of the moment of the shrine's destruction by earthquake, in accordance with the evidence provided by the excavations. The human skeleton was found amongst the stones in the corridor between the doorway of the central room and that of the exit. The bull vase lay behind it.

126. Reconstructed drawing of the decoration of the Kamares ware vase in fig. 127.

127. A unique Kamares ware vase decorated with the plastic figure of a white bull with red markings. Found in the doorway of the central room of the Anemospilia shrine, as depicted in the reconstruction in fig. 125.

tural plan. For instance, the doorway of the west room was not in the middle of the wall, but on the side to the east. Thus this doorway did not correspond to that of the antechamber which consequently looked onto a square pillar partly blocking the room to the west with a thin wall forming a recess. The room's west wall was thicker, while in the corner of the antechamber a stairway had been built. This stairway may possibly have turned left into the thicker part of the wall, and may have led to the room's roof where other rites may have taken place, given that fragments from vases that had fallen from above were found here.

A channel had been carved into the rock around the pillar and in front of the threshold, ending to the west in a small pit dug at the base of the recess. As noted above, the thin wall above the pit under the recess may have borne frescoes on a fine layer of plaster. All the above evidence is more than enough to identify this room with that area of the shrine reserved for blood sacrifices. More especially, the combination of pillars with vats is most common in the so-called «Pillar Crypts», where they would collect the blood of the sacrificed animals.

The same west room proved the poorest in moveable finds. On the other hand, it provided such important information that it is likely to make the discovery of the shrine at Anemospilia one of the most significant, and thus one of the most famous, ever made in Crete. For below the pile of stones from the room's collapsed walls, three more human skeletons were uncovered quite unlike anything that

has come to light from Minoan cemeteries up till now. As we shall see presently, the conditions surrounding the death of these three individuals were so peculiar as to warrant not only the interest of anthropologists, but of various other specialists, not least of the forensic scientist.

More specifically: found in the south-west corner of the room was the skeleton of a woman who had fallen on her stomach with her right hand to her head and her legs apart. This woman was 1.54m. high, about 28 years of age and, as anthropological examination indicated, was a carrier of sickle-cell anemia. A few metres to the north, a second, male, skeleton was found in an even more peculiar position. The man had fallen on his back with his right leg stretched out and his left lifted up at a right angle. Both his arms were folded below the breast. Research indicates that he would have been about 38 years old and 1.78m. high, of exceptionally delicate build but healthy and biologically sound. The forensic scientists termed his pose the «boxer's position», typical of people who are about to receive a blow to the head; they move one leg back

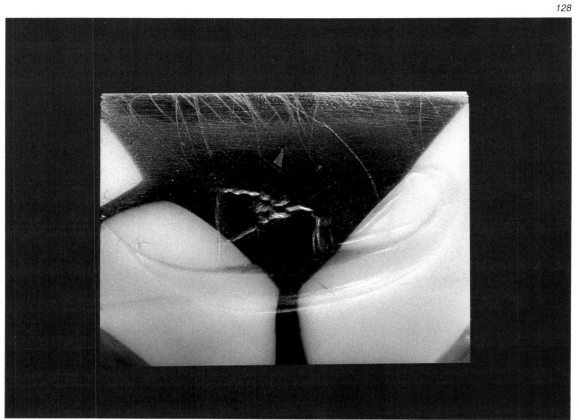

and bring their hands up to protect the head. The tension apparent in the «boxer's position» taken here is clearly due to the fire which forced the arms to contract «due to the prevalence of the bending over the stretching muscles». Thus the cause of death of both these persons, as well as of the third found in the corridor, was due to falling rocks and wood from the roof and the ensuing fire, which at points reached temperatures of 300-500°C thus melting the enamel on some of the teeth.

Items that assist in making some kind of identification of the tall male were fortunately preserved on the skeleton. On his left hand he wore a silver ring covered with iron, quite possibly a signet ring. This is an exceptionally valuable object since in the 17th century B.C. iron would no doubt have been the more precious of the metals, and for this reason covered the silver.

Interestingly, similar rings have been found from a later date, but only in royal tombs. Of similar significance is the achate seal found on his wrist which depicts a ship with a prow in the shape of a bird's head turned backwards. The sailor shown thereon is almost surrealistic, with tension expressed in the exaggerated depiction of the muscles as he rows vigorously. These two personal items are insignia which indicate that the owner must have been a pre-eminent person, a fact underlined by the anthropological examination.

The reconstructions recently undertaken after assiduous examination of the skeletal remains at the Medical School of the University of Manchester by the specialists who had worked on the reconstruction of the head of Philip II of Macedon, prove what the anthropologists had earlier maintained, namely that these were persons of breeding; delicately built but strong. The woman was handsome with a round, smooth forehead and a small, delicate nose. The man seems to have had distinguished characteristics. So as not to risk using more sonorous titles, however, we shall call them here the priestess and the priest.

Apart from the human remains already mentioned, a fourth, male, skeleton was found in the west

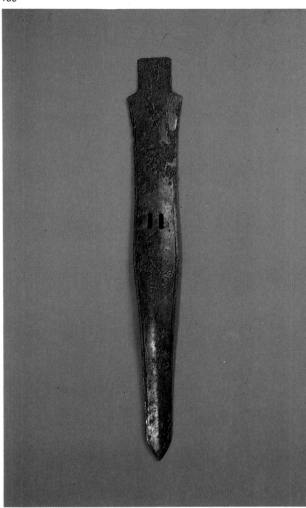

130. The bronze weapon found on top of the third body in the west room, decorated with the head of a hybrid animal.

128. Ornate agate seal-stone with a depiction of a male figure in a ship. Found on the left wrist of the man in fig. 134 in the west room of the Anemospilia shrine.

129. Iron-coated silver ring. Found on the left hand of the man in fig. 134 in the west room of the Anemospilia shrine.

room of the shrine, and in many respects it is this which is the most significant. The fourth body differs markedly from that of the other two in the west room and that in the antechamber. Firstly, it was not located on the floor but on an altar-like structure. Secondly, unlike the others it is not in an outstretched position but was found in a particular stance, and thirdly, a unique bronze weapon was found on the body. These differences indicate that the causes of death here were not the same as those of the others. This will be explained below after careful consideration of a group of pertinent facts.

131. Graphic reconstruction of the Anemospilia shrine (republication from the National Geographic magazine).

132. The two skeletons of the west room as found during the excavations. The female skeleton was found fallen at an angle and face-down in the corner, while the tall male was face-up along the length of the west wall.

The structure on which the skeletal remains of the fourth person were found was a very low trapezoidal base made of stones and clay, and resting on the plaster-covered floor. This permanent fixture was placed not in the centre of the room but to the north-west, behind the pillar. Parallel structures are encountered in low built altars such as that in the west court of the palace at Knossos. The upper surface may have been covered with wood.

The skeleton was found in a diagonal position precisely on top of the altar, turned on its side looking east with the head at the south-east corner; the legs were bent at the knee. A large weapon had been placed obliquely against the belly. In comparison to the other two bodies in the room, these remains were only very lightly disturbed due to the burning of the wooden altar-top on which the body had been laid.

The bronze weapon (0.40m. long) belongs to a very rare type with a short handle and two holes in the middle. The few such weapons that have previously come to light were long classified as knives but recent research does not exclude the possibility that typologically they are, in fact, lances of some description. Depicted precisely in the middle of the lance on both sides is a cast and incised decoration of the head of a fantastic beast with erect ears like butterfly-wings, a long nose, and boar-like tusks. The eyes resemble a fox's while the whole animal is feline in character. Perhaps these various elements had been purposely chosen for symbolic reasons. The heads thus do not constitute a simple decorative motif but should be seen as an emblem.

The death of this fourth person was clearly not occasioned by the earthquake, unlike that of the other three. Anthropological and forensic expertise accustomed to similar circumstances of death was most important here in establishing the actual reasons. It seems that the man's feet had been bound, thus explaining why one ankle abuts the thigh. More importantly, the colour differentiation between the left and right side of the skeleton indicates that the deceased, a male youth of about 18 years of age and 1.65m. high, had lost his blood while still alive. Here, then, we undoubtedly have the remains of a human sacrifice.

This informed observation of the forensic scientists tallies completely with all the circumstantial evidence from the shrine as a whole. According to forensic scientists, death occurred subsequent to the severing of the extended jugular carotid in the left part of the neck. The Minoans knew from bull sacrifices that this was the point from which the most amount of blood could be drawn. The right-handed person who performed the sacrifice could have been the priest, who would have stood behind the victim and made two successive motions, namely the fatal blow followed by laying the weapon down pointing right to left. The earthquake must have occurred after the sacrifice had been performed and prior to any attempt to remove the victim from the altar. The blood which had been collected in the buckets had already been offered to the cult idol, as similar vases found in the central room testify, not to mention the blood-laden Kamares vase depicting a bull, the animal most usually sacrificed.

Human sacrifice, previously unattested in archaeological excavations of Minoan Crete (with a possible exception at Myrtos in Ierapetra from the 3rd millennium B.C.) is, on the other hand, known from

133

134

contemporary practice in Palestine and even in Egypt where it is mentioned in inscriptions. In the prehistoric Aegean, human sacrifices attested in burial finds are cited by Ch. Tsountas (who believed he had found one such instance at Mycenae) as well as by A. Wace, also at Mycenae, and by C. Blegen at Prosymna, W. Vollgraff at Argos, and A. Persson at Dendra. Classical archeologists such as B. Schweitzer were so convinced that human sacrifices were performed that they stated it would only be a matter of time before excavations uncover the necessary evidence. Finally, M. Andronikos believed that the Mycenaeans introduced the custom of human sacrifice into Cyprus. In a Linear B tablet from Pylos, M. Ventris and J. Chadwick identified a reference to a human sacrifice. An important find from Knossos should be mentioned here in relation to this debate: children's bones bearing traces of cutting with a knife which led the excavator to take them for evidence of human sacrifices.

The subject of human sacrifice in ancient Greece is vast, although on vase depictions it is usually de-

133, 134. The heads of the woman and the tall man from the west room of the Anemospilia shrine as reconstructed in clay by the Medical School of Manchester University.

picted by the killing of Polyxena at the tumulus of Patroclus. Studies on the subject found evidence for its widespread practice in the Greek period, for instance at Alos in Thessaly, on Rhodes, at Athens, in Messenia, at Thespiae, Aliartos, Lefkas, Lacedaemonia, Kalydon, Stymphalos, Araphenidae Alei, Orchomenos, Arcadia and elsewhere. Many ancient authors refer to the subject, and not only to the celebrated attempt to sacrifice Iphigenia. The oldest references to human sacrifices exist in Homer where twelve Trojans were offered at the burial mound of Patroclus. Furthermore, two specific historical references are made by Plutarch in his *Life of Themistocles*: the sacrifice of the Messenian captives in 183 B.C. at the tomb of Philopoemen, and the more famous instance on the eve of the battle of Salamis in 480 B.C. where three young captives, the sons of the Persian king's sister San-dake, were sacrificed.

Eminent scholars of Greek religion such as S. Ei-trem, J. Zeihen, P. Stengel and K. Meuli have made detailed studies of human sacrifice and refer to vari-ous types: burial while still alive, throwing into cre-vices, stoning, and (most commonly) killing with a knife attested in Crete, or even with a lance. As far as Crete is concerned, the story of the young Athe-nians sacrificed to the Minotaur suggests the prac-tice of human sacrifice, as does the festival of the Kronia in Cretan Lyktos where human sacrifices are referred to. Finally, the Cretan seer and one of the Seven Sages, Epimenides, was summoned to Athens where he resorted to human sacrifices to rid the city of the curse of Kylon.

Ancient authors agree that human sacrifices were performed for the common good, for victory in war, ritual cleansing, atonement, to make the land fertile, ward off famine and so on. M. Nilsson, the most distinguished scholar of both Ancient Greek and Cretan-Mycenaean religion, maintains that man, when in dire straits, resorts to measures more ex-treme than would be normal, and no sacrifice is so effective as that of a human. He states, furthermore, that «even though most of the examples we know derive from myth, this is so because the idea had a freer rein in the medium of verse from that which it had in actuality where healthy sentiments and hu-manity perceived such aberrations with disapproval and disgust».

Animal sacrifices are known in Crete, with the bull being the most common offering. This seems also to have been the main sacrifice at Anemospilia judging by the special vase with the bull decoration used to gather sacrificial blood. Even here, how-ever, a resort to the ultimate sacrifice was made for the general good, namely to save the area from seismic catastrophe. When the inhabitants left their houses to flee the earthquake, the priesthood re-mained in the shrine at Anemospilia to perform a human sacrifice, the ultimate offering; but in vain.

The human sacrifice attested at Archanes was certainly not a common practice in Minoan Crete, constituting a very rare ritual act. Neither did it occur in the open to public view, but «behind closed doors», such as in the shrine of Lyceus Zeus in Ar-cadia mentioned by Pausanias. Thus the fact that a human sacrifice took place at Anemospilia does not overturn the prevailing image of the peaceful nature of Minoan Crete. But it is no surprise that this nature should include an element of human desperation and self- sacrifice for the salvation of the whole.

Rarely have excavations in so limited an area un-covered such a wealth of evidence as have the in-vestigations of the shrine at Anemospilia.

PUBLICATIONS BY
JOHN AND EFI SAKELLARAKIS
ON ARCHANES (1965-1989)

«Υστερομινωϊκό κενοτάφιο στις Αρχάνες», ΑΔ 20 (1965) 110-18.

«Archanes 1965, Report on the Excavations», Kadmos 4 (1965) 177-80.

«Αρχαιότητες και Μνημεία Κεντρικής και Ανατολικής Κρήτης, 1964», ΑΔ 20 (1965), Χρον. 557-67.

«Die neuen Hieroglyphensiegel vom Phourni, Archanes 1», Kadmos 5 (1966) 109-14.

Found a Gold Ring, Horizon, Winter 1966.
    «The first untouched royal burial found in Crete», The Illustrated London News (March 1966).

«Αρχαιότητες και Μνημεία Κεντρικής και Ανατολικής Κρήτης, 1965«, ΑΔ 21 (1966), Χρον. Β2, 411-19.

«Ανασκαφή Αρχανών 1966», ΠΑΕ, 1966, pp. 174-84.

«Τάφος βασίλισσας στις Αρχάνες», Λεύκωμα Διεθνούς Εκθέσεως Θεσσαλονίκης, 1966, pp. 279-83.

«Ανασκαφές στις Αρχάνες», Αρχιτεκτονική (Aug.-Sept. 1966) 64-7.

«Minoan Cemeteries at Archanes», Archeology 20 (1967) 276-81.

«Mason's marks from Archanes», Europa, Festschrift für Ernst Grumach, Berlin 1967, pp. 277-88.

«Ανασκαφή Αρχανών 1967», ΠΑΕ, 1967, pp. 151-61.
    «Παρατηρήσεις επί της σημειωθείσης εις Αρχάνας ΥΜ ΙΙΙ θυσίας ταύρου», Πεπραγμένα Β΄ Διεθνούς Κρητολογικού Συνεδρίου, Β΄, Athens 1967, pp. 238-46.

«Μινωικές σφραγίδες», Λεύκωμα Διεθνούς Εκθέσεως Θεσσαλονίκης, 1967, pp. 246/7.

«Ελεφαντοστά εκ των Αρχανών», Atti e memorie del 1o Congresso Internazionale di Micenologia, Roma 1968, pp. 245-61.

«Vorpalastzeitliche Siegel aus Archanes», in N. Platon, CMS, II, 1, Berlin 1969, pp. 442-68, n. 379-95.

«Das Kuppelgrab A von Archanes und das Kretisch-Mykenische Tieropferritual», Diss. Heidelberg, PZ 45(1971) 135-218.

«Ανασκαφή Αρχανών 1971», ΠΑΕ, 1971, pp. 276-83.

«Ανασκαφή Αρχανών 1972», ΠΑΕ, 1972, pp. 310-53.

«Αναστηλωτικαί εργασίαι Αρχανών», ΠΑΕ, 1972, pp. 360-62.

«Αποθέτης κεραμεικής της τελευταίας φάσεως των προανακτορικών χρόνων εις Αρχάνας», ΑΕ, (1972), Χρον. 1-11.

«Μυκηναϊκός ταφικός περίβολος εις Κρήτην», ΑΑΑ 5 (1972) 399-415.

«Ανασκαφή Αρχανών 1973», ΠΑΕ, 1973, pp. 167-87.

«Ανασκαφή Αρχανών 1974», ΠΑΕ, 1974, pp. 207-12.

«Ανασκαφή Αρχανών 1975», ΠΑΕ, 1975, pp. 255-321.

«Die Kykladen und Kreta», in J. Thimme, Kunst und Kultur der Kykladeninseln im 3 Jahr. vor. Chr., Karlsruhe 1976, pp. 149-58.

«Ανασκαφή Αρχανών 1976», ΠΑΕ, 1976, pp. 342-99.

«Ανασκαφή Αρχανών 1977», ΠΑΕ, 1977, pp. 459-82.

«Τα κυκλαδικά στοιχεία των Αρχανών», ΑΑΑ 10 (1977) 93-115.

«Ανασκαφή Αρχανών 1978», ΠΑΕ, 1978, pp. 309-22.

«Ανασκαφή Αρχανών 1979», ΠΑΕ, 1979, pp. 331-392.

«Αρχάνες», Σοβιετική Εγκυκλοπαίδεια, Δ, 1979, pp. 3-5.

«Ανασκαφή Αρχανών 1980», ΠΑΕ, 1980, pp. 354-401.

«Gruppen minoischer Siegel der Vorpalastzeit aus datierten geschlossenen Funden», Jahr. RGZM 27 (1980) 1-12.

«Αρχάνες. Ένα νέο μινωικό κέντρο στην 3η και 2η χιλιετία π.Χ.», Δελτίο της Εταιρείας Σπουδών Νεοελληνικού Πολιτισμού και Γενικής Παιδείας 4 (1980) 11-35.

«Ανασκαφή Αρχανών 1981», ΠΑΕ, 1981, pp. 409-48.

«Χρονολογημένα σύνολα προανακτορικών σφραγίδων από τις Αρχάνες», Πεπραγμένα Δ΄ Διεθνούς Κρητολογικού Συνεδρίου, Athens 1981, pp. 510-31.

«Drama of death in a minoan temple», *National Geographic* (Feb. 1981) 205-22.

«Ανασκαφή Αρχανών 1982», *ΠΑΕ*, 1982, pp. 467-530.

«Drama of death in a Minoan Temple», *Reader's Digest* (June 1982) 36-41. This article was published in various languages in all the national issues of the periodical: Greece (July 1982) 74-80, the Netherlands (May 1982) 154-60, Australia (May 1982) 44-8, Finland (May 1982) 69-73, Japan (May 1982) 99-104, United Kingdom (February 1982) 115-19, Portugal (June 1982) 84-9, Canada (January 1982) 77-81, Spain (July 1982) 31-6, Hong Kong (June 1982) 72-7, Switzerland (November 1983) 97-104, Germany (October 1983) 199-205, and Sweden (May 1983) 112-17.

«Ανασκαφή Αρχανών 1983», *ΠΑΕ*, 1983, pp. 367-414.

«Ανασκαφή Αρχανών 1984», *ΠΑΕ*, 1984 (in print).

«Πρωτογεωμετρική-γεωμετρική κεραμεική από τις Αρχάνες» *Κρητ. Χρον.* 26 (1986) 7-50.

«Αρχαιολογική Έρευνα για μιαν αρχαιοκαπηλεία το 1949 στην Κρήτη», *Φίλια Έπη εις Γ.Ε. Μυλωνάν, Β΄*, Athens 1987, pp. 37-70.

«Ανασκαφή Αρχανών 1989«, *ΠΑΕ*, 1989 (in print).

«Archanès à l' époque mycénienne», *BCH* 114 (1990) 67-102.

«Death in Minoan Crete», *ILN* (Spring 1990) 92-3.

«Κεραμεική θαλάσσιου ρυθμού από τις Αρχάνες και η πιθανή ύπαρξη τοπικού εργαστηρίου», *Κρητ. Χρον.* (in print).

«Archanes, Tourkogeitonia, Phourni, Anemospilia», σε G. Cadogan, J.W. Myers, *Aerial Atlas of Crete* (in print).

«Archanes», *Enciclopedia Italiana* (in print).

«Archanes«, *Dictionary of Art* (in print).